The Impact on Consumers of a Restructured Personal Federal Tax

Research for Business Decisions, No. 88

Richard N. Farmer, Series Editor

Professor of International Business
Indiana University

Other Titles in This Series

No. 76 *Management in Post-Mao China:*
An Insider's View   Joseph Y. Battat

No. 82 *Accounting in Developing Countries:*
A Framework for Standard Setting   Felix E. Amenkhienan

No. 83 *The Flaw in Japanese Management*   Haruo Takagi

No. 84 *The Impact of Cybernation Technology*
on Black Automotive Workers in
the U.S.   Samuel D. K. James

No. 85 *Innovative Reporting in Foreign*
Currency Translation   Denise M. Guithues

No. 86 *Productivity versus OSHA and EPA Regulations*   Wayne B. Gray

No. 87 *The Exporting Behavior of*
Manufacturing Firms   Somkid Jatusripitak

No. 89 *Managing the Medical Enterprise:*
A Study of Physician Managers   Carol Betson

The Impact on Consumers of a
Restructured Personal Federal Tax

by
John Huss Green

UMI RESEARCH PRESS

Ann Arbor, Michigan

Produced and distributed by
UMI Research Press
an imprint of
University Microfilms International
A Xerox Information Resources Company
Ann Arbor, Michigan 48106

Library of Congress Cataloging in Publication Data

Green, John Huss, 1955-
   The impact on consumers of a restructured personal
federal tax.

   (Research for business decisions ; no. 88)
   Revision of the author's thesis (Ph.D.—University,
of Pennsylvania, 1984) issued under title: The effects
of alternative personal tax rate structures on savings
and investment.
   Bibliography: p.
   Includes index.
   1. Tax incidence—United States.   2. Income tax—
United States.   3. Consumers—United States—United
States—Econometric models.   4. Flat-rate income tax—
United States—Econometric models.   5. Saving and
investment—United States—Econometric models.   I. Title.
II. Series.
HJ4653.I53G74   1986   336.2'94'0724   85-20980
ISBN 0-8357-1724-0 (alk. paper)

Contents

List of Figures   *vii*

List of Tables   *ix*

1   Introduction   *1*

2   Theory   *7*
     Introduction
     Consumer Theory
     The Aggregation Problem
     Examples of Aggregation
     Exact Aggregation of Demand Systems
     Summary and Conclusion

3   Consumer Demand with Consistent Aggregation   *31*
     Introduction
     Aggregation by Micro Simulation
     An Econometric Model of Consumer Demand
     Structure of Tax Rates
     Income Distribution
     Summary and Conclusion

4   Estimation of an Econometric Model of Consumer Demand   *49*
     Introduction
     Income Distribution
     Personal Federal Taxes
     Consumption Equations
     Demand Equation Method
     Cross Section Model Results
     Summary and Conclusion

5   Historical Simulation and Model Testing   *83*
     Introduction
     Simulation of the Model
     Model Structure
     Historical Simulation
     Sensitivity Analysis
     Ten Percent Increase in Income Simulation
     Income Distribution Parameter Simulation
     Consumer Makeup Simulation
     Ten Percent Reduction in Tax Rates
     Tax Rate Reduction for High Income Taxpayers Simulation
     Redistribution of Tax Rates Simulation
     Summary
     Conclusion

6   Economic Impact of Two Flat Tax Rate Structures   *129*
     Introduction
     Recent Developments in Tax Policy
     Theoretical Links between Tax Rates and Savings
     Tax Rate Links to Savings in the Model
     Tax Policies Considered
     Bradley-Gephardt Proposal
     Pure Flat Tax
     Static Flat Tax Simulation
     Aggregate Savings and Expenditures
     Joint Simulations of a Flat Tax with a Macro Model
     Ex Ante Flat Tax Simulation
     Ex Post Flat Tax Simulation
     Summary and Conclusion

Summaries and Conclusion   *157*
     Alternative Personal Federal Tax Rate Structures
     Theory
     Model Structure
     Empirical Results
     Conclusion

Bibliography   *161*

Index   *163*

Figures

2.1   Fisher Two-Period Model   *10*

4.1   Time Series Estimated Equation — Expenditure Ratio Approach
      64

4.2   Cross Section Expenditure Income Estimated Equations   *67*

4.3   Time Series Estimated Equations — Demand Equation
      Approach   *70*

Tables

4.1   Estimated Parameters for Gamma Income Distribution   *54*

4.2   Effective Tax Rates — 1978   *56*

4.3   Distribution of Tax Return Income — 1978   *57*

4.4   Actual vs. Estimated Aggregate Personal Federal Taxes   *58*

4.5   Expenditure Income Ratios — 1972 Consumer Expenditure Survey   *61*

4.6   Per Capita Price Component of Total Expenditures — Expenditure Ratio Method   *62*

4.7   Actual vs. Predicted Aggregate Real Consumer Expenditures   *65*

4.8   Per Capita Price Components of Expenditures   *68*

4.9   Actual vs. Predicted Aggregate Real Consumer Expenditures   *72*

4.10   Combined Income Distribution Shares for Families and Unrelated Individuals   *76*

4.11   Combined Distribution of Disposable Income Shares for Families and Unrelated Individuals   *76*

4.12   Consumption Shares by Income Level — Total Expenditures as Percentage of Aggregate   *77*

4.13   Consumption Shares by Income Level—Durable Expenditures as Percentage of Aggregate   *77*

4.14   Consumption Shares by Income Level—Nondurable Expenditures as Percentage of Aggregate   *78*

4.15   Consumption Shares by Income Level—Services Expenditures as Percentage of Aggregate   *78*

5.1   Summary of Historical Simulation Errors   *87*

5.2   Aggregate Historical Inputs   *92*

5.3   Selected Aggregate Indicators   *94*

5.4   Combined Income Distribution for Families and Unrelated Individuals   *96*

5.5   Combined Income Distribution Shares for Families and Unrelated Individuals   *98*

5.6   Estimated Aggregate Marginal Propensities to Consume   *102*

5.7   Estimated Aggregate Expenditure-Income Elasticities   *103*

5.8   Summary of Income Distribution Parameter Simulation Results   *109*

5.9   Summary of Consumer Makeup Simulation Results   *111*

5.10   Elasticities Computed in 10 Percent Tax Change Simulation   *114*

5.11   Summary of Results for 10 Percent Tax Cut   *116*

5.12   Summary of Results for High Income Tax Cut Simulation   *117*

5.13   Summary of Results for Tax Shift Simulation   *121*

6.1   Bradley-Gephardt Proposed Tax Rates   *135*

6.2   Personal Federal Taxes—Bradley-Gephardt Simulation   *138*

6.3   Effective Tax Rates — 1978   *140*

6.4   Change in the Distribution of Disposable Income Due to Flat Tax — 1972   *141*

6.5   Change in the Distribution of Consumption Due to Flat Tax — 1972   *142*

6.6   Increase in Aggregate Savings Due to Flat Tax Only   *143*

6.7   Selected Economic Indicators — Ex Ante Flat Tax   *146*

6.8   Components of Gross National Product   *147*

6.9   Sources and Uses of Gross Saving   *151*

6.10   Selected Economic Indicators — Ex Post Flat Tax   *152*

6.11   Selected Components of Gross National Product   *153*

1

Introduction

Taxes on personal income were first levied by the federal government in 1862 as a means of financing the Civil War. The Civil War income tax lapsed ten years later, and a federal income tax was not reintroduced until 1894. However, federal income taxes were ruled unconstitutional in 1895, and not until 1913 did the Sixteenth Amendment to the Constitution give Congress the power to collect taxes on income. In that year, Congress enacted a one percent tax on income between $4,000 and $20,000, with tax rates growing to seven percent on income above $500,000. Personal income taxes have been collected by the federal government continuously since that time.

The structure of the 1913 income tax is very similar to the current system. In 1913, taxes were levied on most types of personal income and tax rates were progressive: low income earners paid no tax and individual rates increased with income. In the current system the tax base also includes most personal income, but there are now many adjustments which can reduce an individual's base income. Tax rates remain progressive, but are now much higher. Before major revisions enacted in 1981, rates ranged from 14 percent to 70 percent.

The concept of progressive tax rates is based on the ability-to-pay principle. The other major basis for tax incidence is the use principle (see Musgrave and Musgrave (1976)). Individuals with higher incomes are assumed to be able to pay a greater percentage of their incomes in taxes. Pechman (1977) supports the ability-to-pay principle and describes the progressive system as "uniquely suited to raising revenue in a democratic country where the distribution of income, and thus the ability to pay, is unequal." A progressive income tax promotes equity across individuals by making disposable incomes more evenly distributed.

However, especially in recent years, the current progressive system has been criticized. One of the main objections is that progressive taxes on income distort incentives to work and save, and the higher the tax rate, the higher the distortion. Critics assert that distortions can be reduced by lowering high marginal tax rates in the current system. Specifically, they argue that by reducing tax rates, individual savings and work incentives would be increased and a higher level of economic activity could result. Proponents of reduced rates believe that gains in aggregate economic activity would outweigh losses in equity from redistribution of income.

The Economic Recovery Tax Act of 1981 addressed the tax rate issue and set in place a 23 percent tax reduction over a three year period. In addition the maximum marginal rate was reduced from 70 percent to 50 percent. Supporters of the measure believed that the tax reductions would cause strong economic growth by increasing personal savings and work incentives. However, for other reasons, including a restrictive monetary policy and a drop in exports, the anticipated gains were not observed. Interest in tax reform to stimulate growth has now shifted to alternative tax rate structures. This study of alternative tax rate structures can thus contribute to the current tax reform debate.

This is a study of the effects of alternative tax rate structures on aggregate personal savings and expenditures. Addressing alternative tax rates is complicated because individual consumers at all income levels need to be studied. Alternative rate structures will result in different changes in tax rates for individuals at different income levels. Therefore, saving and expenditure detail are necessary over the entire income range. For example, one possible alternative to the current system is a flat tax under which all individuals face the same rate. This change would reduce tax rates for high-income taxpayers, and increase rates for low-income earners. In this example, changes in saving and spending patterns are likely to depend on income level, and it is therefore necessary to study consumers at all income levels.

At the individual level, taxes directly affect savings and expenditures in two ways. First, a change in tax rates affects the after-tax return to savings, the incentive to save. Second, taxes affect disposable income which alters the resources individuals have to spend or save. Because these effects can work in opposite directions, a single consumer's response to a shift in tax rates cannot be predicted from economic theory.

At the aggregate level, the impact of an alternative tax rate structure depends on the responses of the individual consumers at each income level, and their relative numbers in the population. For example, if an alternative structure results in higher savings for one income class of consumers and lower savings for another, the aggregate outcome will depend on which group is larger. Therefore, the income distribution — how many consumers are at each income level — must be considered.

We first examine the theory of the consumer and the possible responses of consumer savings to changes in tax rates. We then develop a model of consumer demand which includes the income distribution. The model is used to test two alternative personal tax structures, a flat tax and the Bradley-Gephardt proposal.

Chapter 2 contains the main theory and begins with a review of consumer theory. It shows that high marginal tax rates do not necessarily reduce savings. A negative relationship between marginal tax rates and individual savings is necessary for a reduction in taxes to stimulate savings.

Chapter 2 also shows that most applications of two major aggregate consumption theories, the permanent income hypothesis and the life cycle hypothesis, cannot be used to study a restructuring of tax rates. In most applications of both theories, the methods used in aggregating from micro-economic theory to macroeconomic aggregate equations assume that the distribution of disposable income is fixed. Therefore, the resulting aggregate consumption functions cannot be used to study a restructuring of taxes which alters the distribution of after-tax income. Equations with aggregate income terms and no measure of the distribution of income cannot be used to study alternative tax structures. Both theories, however, can be adapted to study alternative tax rate structures.

Chapter 3 develops the model of consumer demand which combines micro expenditure functions with an income distribution. The result is an advance because it aggregates over individuals consistently and information on individual consumption is not lost. The aggregation process involves simulating micro equations over the distribution of income.

Two approaches to consumer demand are developed in chapter 4. The first, called the expenditure ratio approach, is based on an idea suggested by Lawrence R. Klein (1962). The micro equations are based on ratios of expenditures to disposable income by income class. The second approach, called the demand equation method, uses semilog Engel curves to represent micro behavior.

The model of consumer demand is then estimated in two steps. First, the 1972 Consumer Expenditure Survey (U.S. Department of Labor, 1978) is used to estimate the cross-section micro relationships. These micro equations are then simulated over the income distribution for each year of the historical sample to compute a synthetic variable: the income component of consumption. Then aggregate expenditure and price data are combined with the constructed income components to estimate the price components of consumption.

The historical simulation in chapter 5 shows that the model's prediction of aggregate taxes and expenditures reproduce history closely. Multiplier simulations then test the model's responses to outside shocks. Taxes respond reasonably in the multiplier simulations. For example, the model gives a 15.7 percent increase in taxes for a 10 percent rise in income. This is similar to results reported by Pechman (1977).

The response of expenditures in the multiplier simulations shows that changes in individual disposable incomes dominate the changes in savings and expenditures. The impact of the after-tax rate of return is minimal in the model. Therefore, changes in aggregate savings and expenditures due to alternative tax structures come almost entirely through changes in the distribution of disposable income. Under both alternative approaches to expenditures, low-income consumers exhibit higher marginal propensities to consume than higher-income consumers. Therefore, for example, shifting the distribution of disposable income from low- to high-income consumers will reduce aggregate expenditures even if aggregate disposable income is fixed.

Finally, in chapter 6, two alternative tax structures, a flat tax and the Bradley-Gephardt proposal, are discussed. Both reduce tax rates for high-income individuals and increase the tax base by reducing the value of deductions. The flat tax eliminates all adjustments to income and has one tax rate for all individuals. The Bradley-Gephardt proposal is more complicated and features progressive tax rates in three brackets. Many tax deductions are eliminated, and the value of the remaining deductions is reduced.

The Bradley-Gephardt proposal cannot be simulated exactly in the current model because the model does not explicitly include deductions by income level. Therefore it is not possible to test the exact outcome of the Bradley-Gephardt provisions. However, a tax plan similar to Bradley-Gephardt is simulated to test the impacts of a slightly progressive, simplified tax structure. The tax system studied has almost no distributional impact on after-tax income when compared to the current system. The tax rates in the exercise are very close to the effective tax rates under the current system. Therefore, because expenditures in the model are almost completely determined by disposable income, aggregate savings and expenditures are almost unchanged.

Considering the direct impacts only, a flat tax which generates the same level of collections as in a base simulation causes the level of aggregate savings to increase by an average of 3.7 percent. The increase in savings is due to a decrease in expenditures only because aggregate disposable income is fixed by assumption. Aggregate spending falls because the flat tax redistributes the tax burden. Disposable income is shifted from lower-income individuals who spend a higher proportion of their incomes to lower-spending high-income individuals. Thus, aggregate expenditures drop. However, these results are static and do not reflect the changes in aggregate income which follow a shift in spending patterns.

To show the full economic impact of a flat tax, the income distribution and expenditure model is simulated in conjunction with the Wharton Long-Term model. The joint simulations show that a flat tax reduces aggregate expenditures which in turn causes a drop in aggregate income. The final result shows reduced aggregate income, but a higher level of personal saving. The personal savings rate also increases, but by less than 0.5 percentage points. Despite more savings, the macro simulation also shows a drop in business fixed investment because the lower levels of economic activity require a smaller capital stock. Therefore one of the suggested outcomes of a flat tax — more investment in business capital — is not realized.

2

Theory

Introduction

This chapter reviews some of the literature in consumer theory and the aggregation problem. Consumer theory is discussed because it is through consumer expenditure decisions that tax rates affect savings. The aggregation problem — the link between microeconomic consumer theory and aggregate consumption equations — is presented because it is necessary to maintain information on consumers at different income levels in order to understand the effects of a restructuring of personal federal taxes. Most previous aggregate expenditure studies have eliminated possible distributional effects on personal spending and savings in the process of aggregation by assuming that the distribution of income is fixed or that aggregate expenditures are determined by a population of consumers all with average income.

For the individual consumer, income tax rates affect the expenditure savings decision in two ways. First, taxes reduce disposable income; therefore a change in taxes leaves a consumer with a different amount of income to spend or save. Through the disposable income channel, a consumer will probably increase both current expenditures and savings in response to a tax cut.

Second, taxes alter the after-tax return to savings. This effect works in two ways. The substitution effect reflects a change in the economic rate of substitution of current for future consumption. The income effect accounts for changes in the after-tax interest income from savings received by the consumer. Economic theory presented in this chapter shows that the income and substitution effects are of opposite sign. Therefore, the impact on an individual's savings of a change in the after-tax rate of return depends on the relative strengths of the two effects and cannot be determined by theory.

The aggregation problem is of specific interest because most methods of aggregation eliminate the possibility of examining changes in the distribution of personal taxes through the resulting changes in disposable income and the after-tax rate of return. The resulting consumption equations based on usual aggregation methods depend on aggregate disposable income and other variables. Therefore all tax rate structures which produce the same level of revenue will result in the same level of aggregate consumption. In addition, studies such as Boskin (1978), which include the after-tax rate of return, use an average tax rate, not the marginal rate for each consumer as the theory suggests. This is the result of aggregation.

Two branches of consumer theory are discussed. The first is based on the problem of allocation of resources over time. Discussed in detail are the Ando-Modigliani (1963) life cycle hypothesis, Friedman's (1957) permanent income theory, and a variation of the life cycle hypothesis developed by Tobin and Dolde (1971).

The second branch, demand analysis, considers the problem of allocation of income over commodities, usually in one time period. This approach can be used to study savings by recognizing it as a specific good, future consumption. Demand systems have been based on the problem of allocation of resources over different goods and have often used total expenditures as given. Using total expenditures rather than disposable income is not theoretically necessary. Of specific interest is a demand system developed by Jorgenson, Lau, and Stoker (1981) which attempts to aggregate consistently over individuals.

The study of consumer theory is divided into these branches for convenience. Both areas are based on the same assumptions of consumer behavior. Models which consider the complete allocation problem are reviewed by Phlips (1974).

The remainder of the chapter follows this general outline: Consumer Theory: (a) allocation over time, (b) allocation over goods; the Aggregation Problem: (a) theory, (b) examples in the literature of solutions to the Aggregation Problem.

Consumer Theory

The basis for consumer theory is the assumption that each individual chooses the most preferred bundle of goods available subject to economic constraints. Preferences are assumed to follow certain logical properties so that restrictions on behavior can be developed. If preferences follow these properties, the consumer's problem can be written in terms of a maximization problem. The consumer maximizes a utility function which is an ordinal ordering of his preferences subject to a budget constraint. A general form of the problem is:

$$\text{Max: } u = u (X_1, X_2 \cdots X_n), \tag{2.1}$$

$$\text{s.t. } Y - \sum P_i X_i \geq 0,$$

where X_i = good X_i, P_i = price of X_i, and Y = income.

The consumer formulates a plan for present and future consumption of all goods based on current and expected future prices and incomes. The problem is complicated because the solution gives planned consumption of all goods for the entire time horizon of the consumer. It is further complicated because it depends on expected future income and prices for all goods.

The consumer's problem has been made more manageable by dividing it into two different areas of study. One area is the intertemporal allocation of lifetime wealth where consumption in each period is thought of as one distinct good or as an index of all goods.

The other area is demand analysis where demand for specific goods or systems of demand for all goods are determined for one time period. Future consumption is assumed to be predetermined or represented by savings. When future consumption is predetermined, the demand equations take total expenditures as given. This assumption implies that the consumer solves his problem in two steps. First, he solves the intertemporal problem, and then allocates total expenditures over all goods. This multistep process is suggested by Itzkovich (1978).

Demand analysis can incorporate the intertemporal allocation problem by recognizing that savings is future consumption. This procedure can be made explicit by assuming that savings is a good with a price of the after-tax rate of return, or by determining savings as a residual. As a residual, savings is disposable income less demand for all goods.

Intertemporal Allocation

Two-period model. Allocation of resources over two time periods can be described using a simple Fisher two-period consumption model. The arguments can then be extended to a more complicated multiperiod model. In the simple example, the consumer maximizes his utility by choosing the most preferred levels of consumption in each of the two periods subject to his budget constraint. The budget constraint is the discounted sum of earnings less consumption. Initial wealth and bequests are assumed to be zero. Figure 2.1 shows the typical two-period diagram.

Figure 2.1. Fisher Two-Period Model

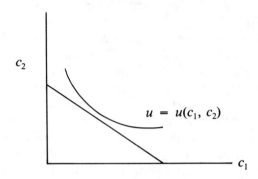

Underlying this diagram is the assumption that the consumer's utility can be described by a function of consumption in both periods. For example,

$$u = u\,(c_1, c_2),\tag{2.2}$$

where c_1 = consumption period 1, c_2 = consumption period 2.

To insure concave isoquants, the marginal utility of consumption in each period must be increasing but at nonincreasing rates. To maximize his utility, the consumer chooses the point where the ratio of marginal utility of consumption in both periods is equal to (minus) the slope of the budget line.

The slope of the budget line is (one plus) the after-tax return to savings. This can be seen from the budget constraint written in terms of period two goods:

$$(c_2 - y_2) = (y_1 - c_1) \cdot (1 + r) \cdot (1 - t),\tag{2.3}$$

where y_i = income in period i, r = rate of return on savings, and t = tax rate.

The left-hand side is excess consumption in period two and the right-hand side is savings from period one in the second period. The slope of the budget line, dropping the cross term, is

$$-(1 + r - t).\tag{2.4}$$

The consumption plan for an individual consumer unit can then be written as

$$c_1 = f(w_1),\qquad(2.5)$$

where $w_1 = y_1 + y_2 / (1+r)$.

In this simple case, the wealth term is the budget constraint, and the consumer's preferences are embodied in the function. A more conventional function can be derived by including the components of the wealth equation

$$c_1 = f(y_1, y_2, rt)\qquad(2.6)$$

where rt = after-tax rate of return.

However, since second period variables are in the future and are unobservable, present period consumption can be explained by making assumptions on how consumers forecast future variables. For example, if a forecast of future disposable income is current disposable income, the consumption function becomes

$$c_1 = f(y_1, rt).\qquad(2.7)$$

This general form can be used to understand the properties of a consumption function derived from Fisher's two-period model. If consumption is a normal good, then an increase in disposable income will cause an increase in consumption. Savings for second period consumption will increase (or become less negative) given an increase in income if the consumer's isoquants are concave and the solution is not at a corner.

The impact of changes in the after-tax rate of return, however, are ambiguous because the income effect and the substitution effect are of opposite sign. Due to the income effect, an increase in the after-tax rate of return shifts the budget line out from the origin for a consumer who is a saver in the first period because returns to first period savings go up. Consumption increases in both periods if it is a normal good. At the same time, due to the substitution effect, consumption falls in the first period and increases in the second because of the change in the slope of the budget line. The increase in the after-tax rate of return raises the price of first period consumption in terms of second period consumption. Hence, the net effect on current consumption is indeterminate.

It is therefore not surprising that past research, which has included the after-tax interest rate directly, has not given conclusive results. Boskin (1978) found a negative after-tax interest elasticity when using a specification similar to equation (2.6). However, Howrey and Hymans (1978) questioned the robustness of Boskin's results. They found that previous results, an insignificant or positive interest elasticity reported by Denison (1958), is probably more likely.

Multiperiod model. The problem of allocation of resources over time has been extended to a multiperiod model by many authors including Ando and Modigliani (1963), Friedman (1957), Tobin and Dolde (1971) and more recently Hall (1978).

The consumer's problem is rewritten as

$$\text{Max: } u = u\,(c_1, c_2 \cdots c_n) \tag{2.8}$$

$$\text{s.t. } \sum_{i=1}^{n} (y_i - c_i)\,/\,\delta_i = 0$$

where y_i is the income in period i,

c_i is the consumption in period i, and

δ is the $\prod_i (1 + rt_i)$, the after-tax discount factor.

The consumer takes income, interest rates, and taxes as given and maximizes over planned consumption.

The multiperiod budget constraint assumes perfect capital markets and, for simplicity, no initial wealth or bequests. It requires that the present value of future income not be less than the present value of future consumption. The budget constraint can be developed from the equation defining the accumulation of nonhuman wealth:

$$Y_t^L + r \cdot w_{t-1} = c_t + \Delta w, \tag{2.9}$$

where Y_t^L is nonfinancial income,

c_t is consumption,

w_t is financial wealth, and

$\Delta w = w_t - w_{t-1}$.

Or, written in first difference form,

$$w_t - w_{t-1} = Y_t^L + r \cdot w_{t-1} - c_t. \tag{2.10}$$

Total wealth valued in period T, the end of life, is

$$w_T = Y_T^L + (1+r) \, w_{t-1} - c_T \tag{2.11}$$

$$= Y_T^L - c_T + [(Y_{T-1}^L - c_{T-1} + w_{T-1} \cdot (1+r)] \, (1+r)$$

$$= \sum_{t=1}^{T} (Y_t^L - c_t) \cdot (1+r)^{T-t}.$$

Discounted to the initial period the budget constraint is:

$$w_o = \sum_{t=1}^{T} (Y_t^L - c_t) \cdot (1+r)^{T-t} / (1+t)^T \tag{2.12}$$

$$w_o = \sum_{t=1}^{T} (Y_t^L - c_t) \cdot (1+r)^{-t},$$

where w_o is the lifetime wealth discounted to initial period.

To measure the effects of a change in interest rates on the individual budget constraint, assume that the individual saves and then dissaves. This pattern is consistent with the idea that the purpose of savings is for retirement. The budget constraint can be rewritten in terms of value at retirement.

$$o = \sum_{t=1}^{R-1} (Y_t^L - c_t) \cdot (1+r)^{R-t} \tag{2.13}$$

$$+ \sum_{t=R}^{T} (Y_t^L - c_t) \cdot (1+r)^{-(t-R)}.$$

The first expression on the right side of equation (2.13) is total savings valued at the age of retirement R. The next expression is total dissavings also valued at age R. The value of savings will increase with higher interest rates because of the increased rate of return on savings. The value of dissavings falls (becomes less negative) because of the higher discount rate. Therefore the budget constraint expands. A net saver can increase consumption in every period because of the increase in interest rates. Correspondingly, a current dissaver who plans to repay debt with future savings will see his budget constraint contract. This is the same result as in the two-period model.

This analysis assumes that the saver does not hold assets in perpetuities or other long-term bonds. If this were the case, an increase in interest rates would cause a capital loss. This would reduce lifetime consumption opportunities (Tobin and Dolde, 1971).

The resulting consumption stream from utility maximization obeys the conditions of the budget constraint and the marginal conditions that the ratio of marginal utility between any two periods is equal to the discount factor between the two periods. For example, Tobin and Dolde write the consumer's lifetime utility function as a weighted sum of utilities in each time period. The utility in a given time period depends only on consumption in that period. Therefore the overall function is separable. The maximization problem is

$$\text{Max: } u(u_1 \cdots u_t) = \sum_{t=1}^{T} u_t(c_t^1 \cdots c_t^n) \cdot 1/(1+\delta)^t \qquad (2.14)$$

$$\text{s.t. } o = \sum_{t=1}^{T} (Y_t^L - c_t) \cdot (1+r)^{T-t}$$

where c_t^1 is the consumption of good 1 in period t and, δ is the time preference factor. The solution of the first-order conditions is that the marginal rate of substitution between any two periods is equal to the market discount rate between the two periods.

$$u'_{t+j}/u'_t = ((1+\delta)/(1 + r))^j \qquad (2.15)$$

where u'_t is marginal utility in period t. The solution to the marginal first-order conditions and the budget constraint is a stream of optimal future consumptions. This can be used to produce a current period consumption equation by assuming that current consumption is in the optimal plan. If conditions change, the consumer reformulates the plan given the new information.

A general consumption function can then be written as

$$c = c(y_1, y_2^e, \cdots, y_T^e, r^e, t^e) \qquad (2.16)$$

where y^e is expected income, t^e are expected future tax rates, and r^e are expected future interest rates.

Consumption is a function of expected lifetime wealth which can be written in terms of current and expected future income, interest rates, and taxes.

There are many ways to rewrite this equation in terms of observable variables. The general approach is to assume that expectations are formed partially distinguishes the different consumption theories, some of which are discussed below.

For discussion purposes, assume that the consumption function is of the form

$$c = f(y,r,t). \qquad (2.17)$$

This assumes that current income, taxes, and interest rates are forecasts of future values. Using this general equation, the effects on current consumption of changes in disposable income and the after-tax rate of return are the same as in the two-period model. An increase in disposable income will increase consumption in all periods. The magnitude will depend on changes in expected future income as well as the specific functional form of the consumption equation. The effects of changes in the after-tax rate of return will be indeterminate because of the opposite signs of the income and substitution effects.

Demand Analysis

In demand analysis, demand equations predict expenditures on specific goods. This approach can be used to determine savings either as a specific good (future consumption) or as a residual category. Demand equations can be used to study the effects of different tax structures by looking at changes in demand for all goods. This approach is included to provide an alternative method of determining aggregate expenditures when the distribution of income is specifically included.

Demand analysis is developed using the utility function which represents a consumer's preference ordering of goods. Demand equations are derived as the solution of the maximization of utility subject to a budget constraint. For a proof of the existence of utility functions, see Varian (1978).

Given the existence of a utility function, the consumer's problem can be represented as a constrained maximization problem:

$$\text{Max: } u(X_1 \cdots X_n) \qquad (2.18)$$

$$\text{s.t. } \sum_{i=1}^{n} P_i X_i \le Y$$

where X_i is good i, P_i is price good X_i, and Y is income.

From the assumptions made on preferences, the resulting utility function is continuous and concave. The solution of the consumer's problem is the solution of the first-order conditions of the maximization. A maximum is assured because of the assumptions on preference. However, since utility is not objectively measured, the problem can be solved for the most preferred bundle of goods. The solution is a set of demand equations of the form

$$X_i = f(P_1 \cdots P_n, Y). \tag{2.19}$$

The properties of this demand equation are (1) homogeneity of degree zero in prices and income; (2) expenditures sum to total expenditures. The budget is exhausted; (3) all demand equations obey the Slutsky substitution properties.

Homogeneity of degree zero in prices and income means that if all prices and income change by the same proportion, demand will not change. In other words, if the price system is renumerated, demand will not change.

The second property is that the budget constraint is satisfied and exhausted. The consumer is never satiated.

The Slutsky equation decomposes changes in demand into two components, price and income effects. The equation as derived by Varian (1978) is

$$\frac{\partial X_j(P, Y)}{\partial P_i} = \frac{\partial h_j(P, v(P, Y))}{\partial P_i} - \frac{\partial X_j(P, Y)}{\partial Y} \cdot X_i \tag{2.20}$$

where h_i is income-compensated demand, and $v(P, Y)$ is indirect utility function.

This equation is important in showing that the compensated own price effect is nonpositive. Regular demand curves are downward sloping except when the income effect is negative and outweighs the substitution effect.

Demand functions can also be derived using the indirect utility function approach. The indirect utility function is the solution to the consumer's maximization problem and is a function which gives the maximum level of utility given prices and income. Using Roy's Identity, demand for good X_i is

$$X_i(P, Y) = \frac{\partial v(P, Y)/\partial P_i}{\partial v(P, Y)/\partial Y}. \tag{2.21}$$

Demand equations can also be directly specified. This ad hoc approach may imply a violation of preference ordering assumptions. However, it can be shown that if the ad hoc demand equation satisfies the Slutsky equation, it can be shown to be consistent with some utility function. This is known as integrability, which means that, if a demand equation satisfies the Slutsky conditions, there is a utility function from which it can be derived.

The Aggregation Problem

The aggregation problem, which in part deals with the link between micro-economic theory and macroeconomic equations, is essential because it is through aggregation that information on individual consumers and their disposable income can be lost.

Aggregation is defined by Green (1964, p. 3) as "a process whereby a part of the information available for the solution of a problem is sacrificed for the purpose of making the problem more easily manageable." Economic theory predicts the behavior of each consumer with respect to every good. In a strict sense, the arguments of each consumer's utility function should be every distinct good and its price for the lifetime of the consumer. Aggregation over goods makes analysis of the consumer's problem more manageable by combining like goods into categories. This limits the number of arguments of individual utility functions and resulting demand functions.

Aggregation over individuals is the process of moving from the micro theory of individual consumers to the observed economy-wide data. It is these aggregates that need to be explained. In the current context, micro theory describes individual consumer behavior while the observed data to be explained are consumption for the economy as a whole.

The results below give the restrictions on individual utility and demand functions necessary for consistent aggregation. Aggregation over goods requires homogeneous separable utility functions. Aggregation over individuals requires that individual demand functions be linear in income or expenditures or, under certain conditions, linear in functions of expenditures. In addition, aggregation causes statistical problems which are reviewed below.

Aggregation over Goods

Green (1964) reviews the conditions necessary for consistent aggregation over goods. Given a utility function of an individual

$$u = u(X_{11} \cdots X_{in_r}, X_{r_1} \cdots X_{rn_r}). \tag{2.22}$$

Each X_{rn} is defined as an elementary good which is the smallest practical grouping where the elements of the group are assumed to be perfect substitutes. The assumption of elementary goods is necessary because no two goods are exactly the same. Green (1964, p. 3) defines consistent aggregation when " . . . the use of information more detailed than that contained in the aggregates would make no difference to the results of the analysis at hand." Consistent aggregation of equation (2.22) requires that

$$u = u(X_1 \cdots X_r) \tag{2.23}$$

where
$$X_1 = f_1 (X_{11} \cdots X_{1_{n_1}}) \tag{2.23_A}$$

Equation 2.23_A is an index function for good category X_i. This function aggregates all of the components of category X_i into one value. Green then proves that the necessary and sufficient condition for equation (2.23) to be a consistent aggregation of equation (2.22) is that the index function (equation 2.23_A) be separable. Separability is defined as

$$(\partial f/\partial X_{r_j}) / (\partial f/\partial X_{r_k}) = f_{r_{j_k}} (X_{r_1} \cdots X_{r_n}). \tag{2.24}$$

This condition means that the index function depends only on the elementary goods in that index.

The assumption underlying consistent aggregation is that the consumer maximizes utility in two steps. First he maximizes a utility function with the quantity indices as arguments. He then allocates each quantity index into its elementary goods. An additional requirement under the two-step assumption is that there exist price indices such that the sum of expenditures on elementary goods in each index category is equal to the expenditure determined in the first level of maximization. This condition can be written as

$$P_{X_r} \cdot X_r = \sum_{j=1}^{n_r} P_{r_j} \cdot X_{r_j}. \tag{2.25}$$

Green proves that this restriction requires that the quantity index functions also be homogeneous of degree one.

Aggregation over Individuals

Aggregation over individuals is the process of moving from micro relationships to the observed macro data which are available as the sum of individual data. For example, if demand for good X by consumer s is

$$X = F_s (Y_s, P) \tag{2.26}$$

where X_s is the demand for good X by consumer s, Y_s is the income of consumer s, and total aggregate demand data to be explained are

$$X = \sum_{s=1}^{n} X_s \tag{2.27}$$

then the desired aggregate equation is

$$X = f(Y,P).$$ (2.28)

Gorman (1953) shows the restrictions under which equation (2.28) is a consistent aggregation of equation (2.26) for all individuals. These restrictions imply that at fixed prices, all individual Engel curves for a given good are linear and parallel. This restriction means that all individual demand functions are linear in income with the same coefficient:

$$X_s = a_s + b \cdot Y_s.$$ (2.29)

Cramer (1969) shows a seemingly easily aggregated consumption function which fits Gorman's general restrictions. The individual's consumption function is:

$$c_i = a_i + b_i Y_i,$$ (2.30)

where c_i is consumption of individual i and a_i, b_i are individual parameters. Because this equation is linear, it can be aggregated by summation

$$\sum_{i=1}^{n} c_i = \sum_{i=1}^{n} a_i + \sum_{i=1}^{n} (b_i Y_i).$$ (2.31)

The left-hand side of equation (2.31) is aggregate consumption. However, the parameters of this equation cannot be estimated from time series data without further assumptions because aggregate income cannot be separated from the term $\Sigma b_i Y_i$.

Cramer then uses what he calls "the primitive assumption" that all of the b_i's are equal. Then equation (2.31) can be estimated in per capita terms using aggregate data. Cramer points out that, in addition to the assumption of equal parameters, this simplification ignores the disturbance term and the proper definition of a population variable.

Even this simple equation cannot be exactly aggregated by summation. Farrell (1953–1954) shows that in the case of linear demand functions exact aggregation is only possible under certain conditions if negative expenditures are not allowed. the argument is extended to consumption functions below. Imposing the nonnegative income restriction gives

$$c_i = a_i + bY_i, \ Y_i \geq -a/b \qquad (2.32)$$

$$c_i = 0, \ Y_i \leq -a/b.$$

Summing over all individuals gives the aggregate equation

$$C = \sum c_i \qquad (2.33)$$
$$= o + \sum (a + bY_i)$$

when $Y_i \geq -a/b$.

This equation is not linear in income and the parameters cannot be estimated from aggregate data.

Cramer also suggests that, rather than assuming that all individual consumption functions have the same parameters, the parameters estimated from a linear function using aggregate data be interpreted as the sample means of the true underlying parameters. This assumption is similar to Phlips's (1974) advice on the aggregation problem. Phlips writes:

> The attitude of most applied econometricians (including myself) is simply to ignore this aggregation problem . . . . When we use aggregate expenditure data divided by population to implement models derived from the theory of the individual consumer, we think of them as relating to the "representative" consumer whose behavior is supposed to reflect the average behavior of the population (pp. 99–100).

If this advice is taken, the distributional effects of tax law changes cannot be studied. Individual consumers are all lumped together as the representative consumer. The linear form imposes identical marginal propensities to consume for given goods on all consumers, which is clearly not supported by data. For example, Prais and Houthakker (1955) found that semilog and log-log Engel curves fit better than linear Engel curves. If Phlips's advice is taken for other functional forms, the effects of income distribution will also be lost because the consumption function of the representative consumer will not be based on consistent aggregation.

Statistical Problems of Aggregation

Even if the parameters of a simple linear consumption function are estimated using least squares from aggregate data, the parameters can be biased. Using a linear demand function as an example, the estimated income term will depend not only on the income parameters of the individual demand equations, but also on the other parameters in the individual equations. This result is shown in matrix form by Theil (1971).

To show the bias, Theil assumes linear functions where each individual function is of the same form, but with variable coefficients. Using matrix notation for the general linear model

$$Y_i = X_i \beta_i + \varepsilon_i \tag{2.34}$$

where Y_i is the column vector of demand for good Y by agent i and X_i is the matrix of explanatory variables for agent i.

The parameter matrix β cannot be estimated because only economy-wide data are observed. Then per capita observations are defined as

$$\overline{Y} = (1/n) \sum_{i=1}^{n} Y_i \tag{2.35}$$

$$\overline{X} = (1/n) \sum_{i=1}^{n} X_i$$

where $\overline{Y}$ is the vector of average consumption of good Y over k years, and $\overline{X}$ is the matrix of explanatory variables averaged over k years.

Average consumption can then be written as

$$\overline{Y} = n^{-1} \sum_{i=1}^{n} X_i B_i + n^{-1} \sum e_i. \tag{2.36}$$

However, the parameters of equation (2.36) cannot be estimated because the x_i are unobserved. However, if all of the corresponding micro parameters are equal, then equation (2.36) can be rewritten as

$$\overline{Y} = \overline{X} \beta + n^{-1} \sum_{i=1}^{n} e_i \tag{2.37}$$

where $\beta = B_i$ for all agents i, by assumption.

Equation (2.37) can be estimated from observed data. However, the parameters are biased. To show this bias, Theil relaxes the assumption that the micro parameters are equal across all consumers. Then the expected value of the parameters estimated from aggregate data can be derived by substituting $\overline{Y}$ from equation (2.37) into the equation for the least squares estimator. Taking the expectation and assuming uncorrelated errors and nonstochastic explanatory variables:

$$\beta_i = (\overline{X}'\overline{X})^{-1}\overline{X}'\overline{Y} \qquad (2.38)$$

$$E(\beta) = (\overline{X}'\overline{X})^{-1}\overline{X}'[n^{-1}X_1 \cdots n^{-1}X_n] \begin{matrix} B_1 \\ \vdots \\ \dot{B}_n \end{matrix}$$

The β_i matrix is the matrix of coefficients resulting from the regression of $\overline{Y}$ on the mean aggregate data $\overline{X}$. Equation (2.38) shows that the parameter β_{xk} estimated using mean aggregate data is a weighted average of the micro parameters b_{xk} and the unrelated micro parameters b_{xj}. Therefore, in the current example, the aggregate marginal propensity to consume is a weighted average of the micromarginal propensities and the other micro parameters in the consumption function. Theil then shows that this result indicates a bias due to aggregation except under very specific conditions.

Examples of Aggregation

In the following sections we outline how two aggregate consumption functions, the life cycle and the permanent income equations, are aggregated from micro theory to the familar aggregate forms, to show what assumptions are necessary for aggregation and whether these consumption functions can be used to study alternative tax structures. Later on, some of Friedman's assumptions which eliminate the income distribution are relaxed to form a basis for a consumption function with the income distribution which is used in this research.

Models developed by Tobin and Dolde (1971), and also by Jorgenson, Lau and Stoker (1981) are then discussed because they include the distribution of income and could be used for a redistribution of taxes.

The Life Cycle Hypothesis

Ando and Modigliani (1963) specifically address aggregation in developing the life cycle hypothesis consumption function, an extension of the simple Fisher model. Assuming that utility is homogeneous in consumption in all periods, and that there are no bequests, the consumption for a consumer unit with head age T in period t is

$$C_t^T = K_t^T \cdot v_t^T \qquad (2.39)$$

where C_t^T is the consumption of family with head age T in period t, K^T is the proportionality factor for family with head age T and v_t^T is the present value of family assets.

Equation (2.39) is expanded to observable data by defining the present value of family assets and average expected future income.

$$V_t^T = a_{t-1}^T + \sum_{\tau=T+1}^{N} Y_\tau^{\varepsilon T} / (1+r_\tau)^{\tau-T} \qquad (2.40)$$

where a_{t-1}^T are assets of family with head age T in period $t = 1$, $Y^{\varepsilon T}$ is the expected income of family with head age T in period t, and N is the final planning period.

Expected future family income is defined as

$$Y_t^{\varepsilon T} = \frac{1}{N-T} \sum_{\tau=T-1}^{N} Y^{\varepsilon T}_\tau / (1+r_\tau)^{\tau-T} \qquad (2.41)$$

where $Y_t^{\varepsilon T}\tau$ is the expectation at time t of income of family with head age T in year τ.

Combining the above three equations gives the consumption function at time t of a family with head age T:

$$C_t^T = K_t^T Y_t^T + K_t^T(N-T)Y_t^{\varepsilon T} + K_t^T a_{t-1}. \qquad (2.42)$$

Ando and Modigliani (1963) aggregate the consumption function in two steps: first within age groups and then over age groups. The age group consumption function is

$$C^T = K_t^T Y_t^T + K_T^T(N-T) Y_T^{\varepsilon T} + K_T^T A_{t-1}^T \qquad (2.43)$$

where T represents age group aggregates.

The community or aggregate consumption function is the sum of the age group functions

$$C_t = \alpha'_1 Y_t + \alpha'_2 Y_t^\varepsilon + \alpha'_3 A_{t-1} \qquad (2.44)$$

where C_t is the aggregate consumption in period t.

Ando and Modigliani show that the parameters of equation (2.44) are stable if three conditions are met. These are (1) the parameters of the age group functions are stable for all groups, (2) the age distribution of the population is stable, and (3) the distribution of income, expected income, and wealth are stable over each age group.

The aggregate consumption function can then be estimated by making one of several assumptions on the formation of expected future income. For example, it can be assumed to be proportional to current labor income.

The key assumptions made for aggregation are the stability of the parameters of equation (2.44) and the fixed age and income distributions.

The stable parameter assumption implies that family units with a head of given age spend the same proportion of their current labor income and wealth as all other family units who have passed or will pass through that age group. This in turn means that all family units have the same utility function and the same expected retirement age and life span.

The assumptions of fixed age and fixed income within age group distributions together imply a fixed income distribution. However, income in this model is net of taxes, and a change in the distribution of disposable income due to a restructuring of tax rates is a violation of the assumptions made in order to move from the theory of the family unit to a model of aggregate data. Therefore the Ando-Modigliani consumption function as aggregated here cannot be used to study changes in the structure of personal tax rates.

Permanent Income Hypothesis

Friedman's (1957) permanent income consumption function is also based on the theory of individual consumer units. Friedman assumes that the permanent consumption of a single unit is proportional to its permanent income where the proportionality factor depends on the unit's wealth, its tastes, and the interest rate it faces.

$$C_P = K(i,w,u) \cdot Y_P \qquad (2.45)$$

where C_P is permanent consumption for an individual, Y_P is permanent income, i is the interest rate, w is individual wealth, and r is the description of individual tastes.

As with the life cycle hypothesis, the consumer unit is assumed to maximize its utility by choosing a consumption path subject to its wealth constraint. Friedman assumes that the optimal path will be "smooth".

Friedman's basic equation differs from the Ando-Modigliani equation for a single unit in several ways. First, Friedman introduces the distinction between observed and permanent income and consumption. In addition, Friedman does not rely on age and expected life span to determine the parameters of the consumption function.

Friedman's approach to aggregation is different from that of Ando and Modigliani. Friedman's first assumption is that the distribution of consumer units can be written as a joint function of (i,w,u,Y_P). The number of consumer units with given characteristics is

$$f(i,w,u,Y_p) \cdot di \cdot dw \cdot du \cdot dY_P \qquad (2.46)$$

with   permanent income $= Y_P + dY_P,$
                 tastes $= u + du,$
                 wealth $= w + dw,$ and
                 interest rates $= i + di.$

Aggregate permanent consumption C_P^* is the integral of the single unit consumption functions over the distribution of consumer units:

$$C_P^* = \int_i \int_w \int_u \int_{Y_P} f(i,w,u,Y_P) \cdot k(i,w,u) \cdot Y_P \cdot di \cdot dw \cdot du \cdot dy. \qquad (2.47)$$

Friedman then assumes that the distribution of consumer units by permanent income is independent of the distribution by the other variables. Therefore the distribution function can then be separated:

$$f(i,w,u,Y_P) = g(i,w,u) \cdot h(Y_P). \qquad (2.48)$$

With this assumption, the aggregate consumption function can be simplified to

$$C_P^* = \int_i \int_w \int_u g(i,w,u) \cdot k(i,w,u) \cdot Y_P^* \, di \cdot dw \cdot du \qquad (2.49)$$

where $Y_P^* =$ aggregate income.

This is possible because aggregate income is defined as

$$Y_P^* = \int_{Y_P} h(Y_P) \, dY_P \qquad (2.50)$$

and the distribution of consumer units by permanent income is independent of the other variables.

Friedman himself questions this assumption:

[The assumption used], namely that the distribution of consumer units by income is independent of their distribution by $i, w,$ and u is obviously false in a descriptive sense. (Friedman, p. 19)

In addition, the assumption of a fixed distribution of permanent income makes it impossible to study changes in the tax rate structure.

Tobin and Dolde Simulation

Tobin and Dolde (1971) develop a model of aggregate consumption based on the life cycle hypothesis. In their paper they study linkages between consumption and monetary policy. Their model uses a very different approach to aggregation than those discussed above. Rather than make assumptions which essentially fix the income distribution, Tobin and Dolde simulate microeconomic consumption functions over a hypothetical population with income and wealth characteristics similar to those of the United States. They assume parameter values for individual family unit consumption functions and evaluate these functions over the range of ages and wealth and income. Aggregate consumption is the sum of the individual consumption functions weighted by age-income distributions similar to the U.S. population.

Tobin and Dolde develop a multiperiod consumption model based on Fisher's two-period model. Each consumer plans current and future consumption to maximize his or her utility subject to a wealth constraint. This is similar to the model of Ando and Modigliani. Tobin and Dolde, however, specify an exact functional form of the utility function

$$u(c_0, c_1 \cdots c_T) = \sum_{i=0}^{T} u(c_i) \cdot (1+\delta)^{-i} \tag{2.51}$$

where δ is the subjective discount factor.

Because the time preference term is separated from the utility function in each period, the optimal consumption path will obey the marginal condition

$$u'(c_i)/u'(c_{i+1}) = (1+\delta)/(1+r). \tag{2.52}$$

Equation (2.52) results in a smooth consumption path if the subjective rate of time preference equals the economic discount rate.

Tobin and Dolde develop consumption equations for two cases, with and without a liquidity constraint. The liquidity constrained case faces a lower limit on savings due to forced savings such as mortgage payments and insurance policies. In both cases the consumer unit consumption function is of the form

$$c_i = f(y_i, w_i, r). \tag{2.53}$$

This equation with assumed parameter values is then evaluated and summed over the range of ages 21 to 85 using a wealth-income profile similar to that in the United States.

The coefficients of the consumption functions are not obtained econometrically. Rather, they are specified such that predicted aggregate consumption would be close to observed values.

Alternate scenarios which affect the age and wealth groups differently can then be studied using this method of micro simulation. Tobin and Dolde look at a variety of different scenarios which are assumed to be the result of actions by the monetary authority. They study tax policy by imposing a proportional tax change on all groups.

This approach of micro simulation does allow the investigation of problems affecting individuals distinguished by age, wealth, income, or other characteristics which would otherwise be lost in aggregation. Tobin and Dolde were able to examine wealth specific problems because their micro theory model of consumer behavior included wealth and it was preserved in aggregation by simulation.

The model developed in this dissertation also aggregates by simulation of micro consumption functions. However, we study the effects of a redistribution of personal income taxes and therefore the microequations are simulated over the income distribution. Including a link to the distribution of wealth is a topic for future research.

Exact Aggregation of Demand Systems

Jorgenson, Lau and Stoker (1981) develop an econometric model of demand which is based on exact aggregation over individuals. The model assumes that each individual allocates shares of total expenditures according to the translog indirect utility function. Using vector notation, this indirect utility function can be written as

$$\ln V_k = \ln P' \left(\alpha_p + \tfrac{1}{2} \beta_{pp} + \beta_{pA} A_K \right) - \ln M_k {\cdot} D_k \qquad (2.54)$$

where
V_k is indirect utility function of consumer k,
A_K are attributes of consumer k,
P is the vector of prices,
M_k are expenditures of consumer k, and
$D_K = i'\alpha_P + i'\beta_{pp} \cdot \ln P/M_k + i'\beta_{pA} \cdot A_K$.

The vector of expenditure shares for consumer k is derived by Roy's identity

$$W_K = 1/D_K \left(\alpha_p + \beta_{pp} \cdot \ln P/M_K + \beta_{PA} \cdot A_K \right) \qquad (2.55)$$

where W_K is the expenditure share vector for consumer k.

The theory of exact aggregation as developed in Jorgenson, Lau and Stoker requires that the individual share equation be linear in functions of individual expenditures and attributes. This condition is satisfied if the denominator of equation (2.55) does not include individual income or attributes. This holds when

$$i' \, \beta_{pp} i = 0 \quad \text{and} \quad i' \, \beta_{PA} = 0. \tag{2.56}$$

The economy-wide share of aggregate expenditures for a given good is the sum of individual expenditures of that good over total expenditures. The vector of aggregate expenditure shares is then

$$w = (1/D) \, (\alpha_p + \beta_{pp} \ln P - \beta_{pp} \cdot i \cdot (\Sigma \, M_K \ln M_K / \Sigma M_K) \tag{2.57}$$

$$+ \, \beta_{PA}(\Sigma M_K A_K / \Sigma M_K)$$

because α_p, β_{pp}, and β_{PA} are constant matrices. Therefore the aggregate share of a given good depends on the distribution of total expenditures through the term which sums the weighted logs of expenditures. Therefore, a change in the distribution of total expenditures affects the aggregate (and individual) expenditure shares.

Jorgenson, Lau and Stoker use cross section data to estimate the β_{pp} and β_{pA} parameter matrices. The remaining parameters are estimated using time series price data. They use the model to evaluate the welfare implications of the oil price shock using the necessary compensating variation as measured by the translog indirect utility function.

In Jorgenson, Lau and Stoker a more complete model of consumer demand based on the same theory of exact aggregation is presented. One difference in the two papers is that in the second paper total expenditures by income level are determined using the distribution of income, a tax rule, and a consumption function. This would allow the effects of a change in the tax structure to be studied. However, details on how this is done are not spelled out.

Summary and Conclusion

The consumer theory presented above gives two methods for determining an individual's consumption. The first method is based on the solution to the intertemporal allocation problem and results in a general consumption function for the individual which depends on his initial wealth, his income, the interest rates he faces, and taxes. The second method is developed from the static theory of the consumer. Demand equations for different groups of goods are developed and the sum of these demands determines total consumption. The major difference is that the demand equations do not depend on the individual's wealth, but only on his income and the prices and taxes he faces.

In both methods, the theory is based on the individual consumer and therefore yields microeconomic relationships. However, to make inferences at the macro level, it is necessary to aggregate over individual consumers.

To aggregate consistently, it is shown that the micro functions must be linear in income or functions of income. The methods of aggregation for several well-known aggregate consumption functions are shown. Of these, only the linear Keynesian equation can be said to be based on consistent aggregation. However, the micro equations underlying the Keynesian aggregate function cannot be supported by the data.

Jorgenson, Lau and Stoker present a consistently aggregated demand system. However, it relies on the distribution of total expenditures as given and therefore cannot be used to study total consumption expenditures. Tobin and Dolde determine aggregate consumption using the method of micro simulation. In this way they preserve the hypothesized underlying micro relationships. A similar method is developed in the next chapter.

3

Consumer Demand with Consistent Aggregation

Introduction

This chapter continues to develop the two models of consumer behavior. Previously, the theory behind equations to explain total expenditures and also demand for specific goods by individual consumer units was developed. In addition, methods of aggregation which allow microeconomic relationships to be applied to observed aggregate data were discussed. This chapter focuses on alternative aggregation procedures which are less restrictive than most used in the past. The result will be two models of consumer expenditures which incorporate consistent aggregation. The models will be used to study the effects of a redistribution of disposable income on consumer expenditures.

The two competing models of consumer spending differ in theoretical derivation and degree of disaggregation of goods explained. The first model predicts total expenditures while the second predicts demands for specific goods which sum to total expenditures. In both cases, savings can be determined as the difference between disposable income and expenditures. Although both models can be used to study consumption and savings, the second model can also be used to study the effects of changes in the distribution of income on the demand for different goods.

As was shown in chapter 2, consistent aggregation over individuals requires that the aggregate consumption or demand equations be linear in income or functions of income. However, equations which are linear in income are inconsistent with observed declining marginal propensities to consume as income rises. Therefore, other methods of aggregation should be considered.

Tobin and Dolde use micro simulation to aggregate over individuals. They specify consumption equations for individuals and simulate them over an income-wealth distribution with characteristics similar to the U.S. population. A similar approach which results in equations which are linear in functions of income is developed here. The major advantage is that the structures of equations for individuals can be preserved and aggregation is consistent.

The aggregation technique used can be traced to Klein (1962), who proposed using income distributions to determine aggregate consumption. This idea is shown to be consistent with Friedman's (1957) permanent income model by relaxing some of Friedman's aggregation assumptions.

Estimation of the system requires pooling cross section and time series data. Although for a different purpose, Stone (1954) formed consumption equations by combining an income term parameter estimated from cross section data with a price term estimated from time series data. A similar technique is used here.

The aggregation technique developed here requires that the distribution of disposable income be known. Therefore, a model of the distribution of income for consumer units which is based on the gamma density function is developed. In addition, a model of tax rates by income level is discussed.

Aggregation by Micro Simulation

Rather than using aggregate consumption or demand equations which are based on the representative consumer assumption, this paper aggregates over consumers by directly adding up consumption of individuals at all levels of income. If aggregate demand for good X is defined as the sum of demands for good X by all consumers, then aggregate demand can be expressed as

$$X = \sum_{i=1}^{n} X_i = \sum X_i (Y_i, P). \tag{3.1}$$

The idea of summing over individuals was proposed by Klein (1962) in the context of total expenditures. He suggested combining knowledge of the income distribution with expenditure income shares by income class. Rather than assuming a representative consumer for the entire economy, Klein assumes a representative consumer for each income class. Total expenditures are calculated as

$$E = \sum_{i=1}^{R} E_i \qquad (3.2)$$

$$= \sum_{i=1}^{R} e_i \cdot \overline{Y}_i \cdot N_i$$

where e_i is the ratio of expenditures to income in income class i, $\overline{Y}$ is average income in income class i, N_i is the number of consumers in income class i, and R is the number of income classes. The ratios of expenditure to income, e_i, and average income in the income classes, $\overline{Y}$, can come from a single cross section budget study. Klein suggests that per capita expenditures in each class can be interpreted as permanent expenditures because they are estimated from cross section data which does not suffer from fluctuations over time. Cross section data represent a fixed point in time and are averages of micro data. Therefore cross section data represent the behavior of consumer units over the range of income levels.

The number of consumer units in the income classes can be taken from yearly income distribution surveys such as those available from the tax authorities in income tax reports. Aggregate income can then be allocated into income cells over the historical sample period using the income distributions. Aggregate expenditures are then computed for each year by applying the single set of expenditure ratios to the income distribution in each year. Aggregation is accomplished without the representative consumer assumption for the aggregate economy. Representative consumers are still assumed for each income cell. This procedure can be considered aggregation by simulation in that expenditure-income shares from one budget study are simulated over the income distribution for each year.

Demand equations can also be aggregated by simulation. Rather than using fixed expenditure shares for each income cell, expenditure-income functions can be estimated from cross section data. The cross section equation can be simulated over the income range and then the resulting expenditures by income level can be aggregated using the income distribution. Price effects can then be estimated in a second step. This idea is developed below.

Aggregation by micro simulation as developed here has the advantage that the structures of the individual consumption and demand equations are preserved. This allows the distribution of income and therefore the personal tax structure to play a part in the determination of aggregate consumption.

An Econometric Model of Consumer Demand

Two different approaches to consumer demand into an econometric model are developed to determine consumer demand using two methods which can be used to test the effects of a restructuring of personal federal tax rates. To be useful, the model must not only be consistent with the theory discussed above and the observed data, but also incorporate key aspects of the tax law which are under consideration for change.

The first approach, the expenditure ratio method, is a direct application of Klein's method and can be used to study the effects of a redistribution of disposable income on consumption and savings directly. The second approach makes use of demand equations for several categories of goods which sum to total expenditures. This model can be used to study shifts in demand for specific goods as well as changes in total spending and savings. Because each can serve different purposes, both are developed.

In addition, the two approaches to consumer spending differ in results. As will be discussed later, applications of both predict aggregate expenditures well over history. However, multiplier simulations will show that the two approaches respond very differently to income shocks.

Estimation

Direct estimation of consumption functions which are to be aggregated by simulation would require a cross-sectional sample of individuals over time which is called a panel study. Estimation requires variation of consumer income and demand and also variation of prices. Consumers' incomes vary in cross-sectional samples and prices vary over time. Since an appropriate panel study is not available, an alternative to direct estimation is necessary. One possibility is pooling cross section and time series data from different sources.

Stone (1954) first pooled the two different data types. He used cross-sectional budget study data to estimate income elasticities and used the resulting estimated parameters in time series equations to estimate price effects. His reason for this procedure was to eliminate problems caused by the collinearity of price and income data. Collinear explanatory variables result in large variances of least squares parameters. This method of combining cross section and time series data involves the use of extraneous information about the income coefficient. The information is extraneous in that it comes from a different sample. For a discussion of extraneous information and the associated statistical problems, see Durbin (1953).

Stone used a two step process to combine the cross section and time series data. He first used the cross section data to estimate the income coefficients by estimating consumption income functions, or Engel curves. He then simulated these functions over time, replacing aggregate income as the income variable. This calculation formed a synthetic income component of consumption over time. In the second step he explained aggregate consumption with this synthetic income component of consumption and relative price terms.

In this study, cross section and time series data are combined in order to insure consistent aggregation. The estimation process is similar to Stone's two step procedure, but with one major modification which preserves consistent aggregation. The first step is to use cross section data to estimate individual consumer unit consumption-income functions. These equations are then simulated over the full income range and the resulting expenditures at each level of income are summed using the income distribution to weight the results. The procedure results in a synthetic variable which is the income component of consumption and is similar to Stone's synthetic variable. However, in this case individual consumer units are summed explicitly, eliminating the need for the average consumer assumption in aggregation. The price component can then be estimated in a second step where aggregate expenditures are explained in a regression by the synthetic income variable and price series. The actual process is explained in detail below for both the expenditure ratio and the demand equation approaches.

Ordinary least squares can be used to estimate the coefficients in both the cross-section demand equations and time series equations. The optimal properties and necessary assumptions concerning the error terms of least squares estimation are well known. However, one possible violation of these assumptions occurs because it is reasonable to assume that the variance of individual demand in the cross section sample increases as income rises. Therefore it is possible that the errors will not be homoskedastic. This problem is discussed in the estimation section of chapter 4 where a generalized least squares approach is tried but rejected because of unreasonable results.

Functional Forms

The method of estimation, along with consistent aggregation, places some restrictions on possible functional forms. The major restriction is that the left-hand side of the equation, consumption, must be normalized to consumption only. The right-hand side can then be any separable function of income and prices. The individual functions must be of the form

$$c_i = f(Y_i) + g(P). \tag{3.3}$$

Aggregate consumption is then expressed as

$$C = \sum_{i=1}^{n} c_i = \sum_{i=1}^{n} f(Y_i) + \sum_{i=1}^{n} g(P). \qquad (3.4)$$

The separability assumption allows the income term $f(\cdot)$ to be estimated from cross section data alone under the assumption that prices are the same for all consumers in a cross section study. The price function $g(\cdot)$ can then be estimated from time series data after the income component has been removed.

The major assumptions underlying this approach are that the consumption and demand functions can be written in the form of equation (3.3) and that preferences are stable over time. The general form requires that consumption and demand equations are separable in income and prices. It also implies that preferences are identical over consumers. The functions $f(\cdot)$ and $g(\cdot)$ are not subscripted. This restriction could be relaxed by assuming that preferences are related to observable attributes as is done in Jorgenson, Lau and Stoker (1981), who link preferences to demographic characteristics. This is discussed in chapter 4.

Even with the restrictions of consistent aggregation imposed, there are many possible functional forms for both the total consumption function and the demand equations. The choices can be narrowed by deriving forms from specific utility functions or by taking functions from the literature.

Total Expenditures

Deriving a functional form for an individual's total consumption from a specific utility function would be difficult because the resulting equation would have many expected future variables as arguments. This complication comes from the fact that current period consumption is part of a lifetime optimal consumption plan. Chapter 2 shows that the first-order marginal conditions equate the marginal rate of substitution between consumption in each period. Therefore current period consumption depends on expected future consumption. Choosing a functional form from the literature might be a better approach.

Using Friedman's permanent consumption model is possible because it can be applied and has been shown to be consistent with utility maximization. Yaari (1976) shows the conditions under which the permanent income hypothesis is valid. Yaari assumes that the consumer's problem is to maximize the expected sum of future utilities given a wealth constraint. He further assumes that the consumer faces a zero interest rate and has a zero subjective discount rate. In addition, the consumer does not know with certainty his future incomes. The result is that, as the number of time periods tends to infinity, the optimal consumption in any period is

$$c^* = u = \frac{1}{N} \sum_{t=1}^{T} Y_i. \tag{3.5}$$

If the consumer estimates his permanent income as u, then the permanent income hypothesis, which is defined by

$$c_P = k_i(r,w) \cdot Y_P, \tag{3.6}$$

holds with $k = 1$.

Yaari's results imply that k_i is equal to one for all consumers. However this is not supported by the data. One possible approach is to estimate k_i from cross section data. This is exactly Klein's (1962) suggestion as a solution to the aggregation problem. Consumption expenditures for each income class are then expressed as

$$c_K = a_K \cdot (Y \cdot (1-t(y))) \tag{3.7}$$

where c_K is the consumption in income class k, and a_K is the expenditure-to-income ratio.

Aggregate consumption is then

$$c = \int_Y a_K(Y) \cdot (Y \cdot (1 - t(Y))dY \tag{3.8}$$

where a_K are expenditure-to-income ratios. In this form, the coefficient $a(y)$ is a function of income and can be estimated from a cross section budget study either as a continuous function or as a step function.

A further justification for this approach can be found by relaxing some of the assumptions Friedman (1957) used in aggregating the permanent consumption function from the micro theory to his familiar aggregate consumption equation. Recall that an intermediate step in the development of the aggregate equation is

$$c_P^* = \int_i \int_w \int_u \int_{Y_P} f(i,w,u,Y_P) \cdot K(i,w,u) \ Y_P \cdot di \cdot dw \cdot du \cdot dY_P. \tag{3.9}$$

Total permanent consumption is the summation of consumer unit consumptions over all consumer units. The distribution of consumer units is assumed to be conditional on permanent income, tastes, wealth and interest rates. In this form the function $f(\cdot)$ is a size distribution, not a probability distribution. (The integral of $f(\cdot)$ over all variables equals the total number of consumers, not one.)

Friedman's next step is to assume that the distribution of consumers can be separated as

$$f(i, w, u, Y_p) = g(i, w, u) \cdot h(Y_p). \tag{3.10}$$

This implies that the distribution of consumers' income is independent of all other variables including wealth.

Friedman then assumes that the distribution of income is fixed over time. This assumption eliminates the possibility of using Friedman's approach to the aggregate consumption equation to study a redistribution of personal taxes. An alternative assumption is that the distribution of consumers by income is not fixed but the distribution by preferences and wealth are fixed and uniform. Alternatively, the other variables can be assumed not to enter into the determination of $k(\cdot)$. This is a strong assumption and could be relaxed. The wealth issue is considered by Tobin and Dolde (1971). The preference restriction is relaxed by Jorgenson, Lau, and Stoker (1981). Further assume that all consumers face the same interest rate, which is equivalent to assuming that the distribution of consumers by interest rates is uniform. This assumption will be relaxed later in the context of after tax rates of return. Under these assumptions, aggregate consumption becomes

$$c_P^* = \int_{Y_P} Y_P \cdot f(Y_P) \cdot K(Y_P) \, dY_P. \tag{3.11}$$

Micro simulation can be used to calculate total consumption. If the function $k(\cdot)$ and the distribution of income are known, aggregate consumption can be calculated by evaluating the integral in equation (3.11) over the entire income range.

This idea can be extended to include personal taxes explicitly. Micro simulation is ideally suited to this because personal federal tax rates are a function of income. Equation (3.11) becomes

$$c_P^* = \int_{Y_P} Y_P \, (1 - t(Y_P)) \, K(Y_P) \, dY_P. \tag{3.12}$$

Permanent income is replaced by after tax permanent income which is defined as

$$Y_P' = Y_P \, (1 - t(Y_P)). \tag{3.13}$$

The progressive tax structure is explicitly included in the aggregate consumption equation. This is essential for alternative tax structure simulations.

A strict interpretation of this approach requires knowledge of permanent income and consumption which are unobservable. On an individual consumer unit basis, one might expect larger transitory components of income at the extremes of the distribution. However, the average income and expenditures in the cross section income cells can be interpreted as long-run permanent observations.

A possible elaboration of this model is to assume that the income coefficient term is also a function of the after-tax rate of return to savings. This is similar to Friedman's original model.

The after-tax rate of return is of special interest because it has been the focus of past research and is a major argument for a restructured tax system. Examples in the literature are found in Boskin (1978) and in Howrey and Hymans (1978). These papers found, respectively, negative and positive after-tax rate of return effects.

Both of these studies suffer from misspecification and aggregation problems in that they use an average tax rate in aggregate consumption/savings equations.

Unfortunately, an equation containing an after-tax rate of return term cannot be estimated using the pooling technique outlined above. The marginal tax rates vary by income and therefore parameters associated with the after-tax rate of return must be estimated in the cross section step. However, market interest rates vary over time. The $g(\cdot)$ function in equation (3.10) which contains price effects cannot be separated from the income term.

However, the question of rate of return effects need not be discarded. An alternative is sensitivity analysis which can establish a range of likely outcomes through the after-tax rate of return. The idea is to specify different rate of return elasticities and test their impact on aggregate consumption. This approach can answer the question of how large the rate of return elasticity must be to produce a given change in savings. It cannot determine the size of the elasticity.

Demand Equation Model

One approach to arriving at a functional form for demand equations is direct specification. The other approach is to derive demand equations from a specific utility function. The advantages of direct specification are that the demand equations are insured to fit the form necessary for consistent aggregation and the parameters can also be estimated. The equations can then be checked for consistency with consumer theory.

One possible specification is

$$X_i = a + b \cdot \ln Y_i + c \cdot \ln P \tag{3.14}$$

where P represents all prices. This fits the aggregation requirements of equation (3.3) and can be estimated using a version of Stone's pooled data method.

The income parameter can be estimated from a cross section sample alone. The necessary assumption is that all consumers in the cross section sample face the same prices. Therefore there is no price variation. The estimated equation becomes

$$X_i = a + b \cdot \ln Y_i. \tag{3.15}$$

Equation (3.15) is a semilog Engel curve which was tested by Prais and Houthaker (1955).

Given the estimate of the income parameter, an intermediate variable similar to Stone's synthetic variable can be constructed. It is the income component of the aggregate demand for good X:

$$Z_t = \int_Y [a + b \cdot \ln \sum Y \cdot (1 - t(Y))] \, f(y) \, dy. \tag{3.16}$$

The income distribution for each year is explicitly included. In addition, the tax structure for each year is included.

The price parameters can then be estimated by the regression

$$X_t - Z_t = c \cdot \ln P. \tag{3.17}$$

The left-hand side is total demand for good X net of its income component. The right-hand side is the price component and can be expressed in practice as the price of good X relative to an index of other prices.

The next problem is to show the properties of equation (3.14) and that it is consistent with consumer theory. A demand function need not be derived from an exact utility function to be consistent with consumer theory. Instead, the function can be shown to follow the restrictions imposed by theory which were already reviewed.

Homogeneity of degree zero in prices and income means that if all prices and income change by the same percentage, demand for good X does not change. This can be shown using Euler's theorem for showing the homogeneity of an equation. Rewriting equation (3.14) and defining y as real income (y/p) yields

$$X_i = a + b \cdot \ln (Y_i/P) + c \cdot \ln (P_i/P). \tag{3.18}$$

Taking the total derivative

$$dx_i = b \frac{dy}{Y} + c \frac{dP_i}{P_i} - (b + c) \frac{dP}{P} \qquad (3.19)$$

$$= 0 \text{ (when nominal income and all prices change}$$
$$\text{by the same relative amount)}$$

shows that the equation is homogeneous of degree zero.

The added condition requires that the sum of expenditures of all goods does not exceed total income. This condition depends on the estimated parameters and the results from chapter four indicate no problems.

The properties of equation (3.14) are easy to derive. The marginal propensity to consume for a consumer unit with income y_i is

$$dX_i/dY_i = b \cdot 1/Y_i. \qquad (3.20)$$

Therefore the marginal propensity to consume good x declines as income rises. This is consistent with empirical observation.

The consumption-income elasticity also depends on the level of expenditures. It is

$$\varepsilon = b \cdot 1/X_i. \qquad (3.21)$$

The demand-income properties for aggregate demand depend on the income distribution and therefore an analytic solution does not exist. However the response of aggregate demand due to income shocks can be studied with the completed model. This will be developed in chapter 5.

The semilog form of equation (3.14) is not the only possible specification. For example, a quadratic equation can be interpreted as a Taylor series expansion of the underlying function. A quadratic form was estimated and, although the regression test statistics were superior to those resulting from the semilog form, the estimated parameters imply unrealistic results such as declining and negative consumption at high income levels. The details are given in the estimation section of chapter 4.

Structure of Tax Rates

Up to this point, tax rates have been written in a general way as a function of income, $f(y)$. This section explains how personal federal taxes are to be modeled.

The actual federal tax law is complex. Tax tables which depend on marital status are applied to an individual's taxable income. Taxable income is defined as most money income less personal exemptions and deductions. The amount of a taxpayer's personal exemption is based on the number of dependents claimed, with additional exemptions for the elderly and blind.

Deductions are a standard amount, depending on marital status, or are itemized by the taxpayer. The major itemized deduction categories are for interest charges due to mortgage payments and other taxes. (See Pechman (1977).)

The ideal tax model would reproduce the tax law exactly. It would include distributions of income by income type and filing status. It would also incorporate a method of determining the distribution of deductions and exemptions by income.

A practical alternative is to construct an effective tax table where the effective tax rates are based on adjusted gross income rather than on taxable income. The idea is to construct a table of rates which has the same progressive structure as the current tax statute. The major differences are that there will be one effective tax table rather than four tables. In addition, the effective rates will be applied to adjusted gross income rather than taxable income. It will therefore take account of deductions and exemptions.

The effective tax rates can be derived from the annual series of IRS publications, "Survey of Income Statistics". These publications contain taxes paid and income earned by adjusted gross income class. From this the average tax rate for each income class can be calculated. Then the effective marginal rates can be derived by solving the definition for average tax rate:

$$AR_i = \frac{AR_{i-1} \cdot B_{i-1} + (B_i - B_{i-1}) \cdot MR_i}{(B_i + B_{i-1})/2} \tag{3.22}$$

where AR_i is the average rate in bracket i, MR_i is the marginal rate in bracket i, and B_i is the upper income limit in bracket i, for the marginal rate. The numerator of equation (3.22) is the total taxes collected in bracket i and the denominator is the midpoint income. The result is a tax table with the same structure as the current law with increasing marginal tax rates.

The effective rates are average in that they combine the different tax rates paid by taxpayers of different marital status. They are simplified by including reductions in taxes paid due to income reductions as a result of exemptions and deductions.

This approach has the advantage that changes in the tax structure can be studied. A general change affecting the structure of the different tax tables in the same way can be directly applied to the effective tax rates.

A more complex change in the statutory rates can be simulated by first calculating the implied changes in the effective tax rates. For example, assume that a change in deductions is to be examined. Further assume that there is only one set of statutory rates and that there are no exemptions. The implied changes in the effective rate structure can be seen by deriving the relationship between the statutory rates and the effective rates. Then, in a given tax bracket, taxes are defined as

$$\text{TAX} = \text{SR} \cdot (Y\text{–}D) \qquad (3.23)$$

where TAX is tax paid by taxpayer, SR is the statutory rate, Y is adjusted gross income, and D are deductions. The effective rate is defined as

$$
\begin{aligned}
\text{ER} &= \text{TAX}/Y \qquad\qquad\qquad (3.24) \\
&= [\text{SR} \cdot (Y\text{–}D)]/Y \\
&= \text{SR} - \text{SR} \cdot D/Y
\end{aligned}
$$

where ER is the effective rate. The effective rate is the statutory rate corrected by the deductions to income ratio.

In this way the new effective tax rate structure can be developed. Other tax policy alternatives can be simulated in similar ways.

Income Distribution

In the development of the tax and consumption models, the distribution of income has been used and assumed to be known. The distribution of income is an integral part of consistent aggregation of consumer demand. Rather than assume as a method of aggregation that all consumers have identical incomes equal to average income as many previous studies have done, this study uses the income distribution so that the income level of each consumer is known. Therefore, individual consumption can be determined as a function of the individual's income. Aggregate consumption can then be the sum of each individual's consumption.

The beginning of this chapter reviews Klein's (1962) suggested approach for aggregation over consumers. The suggestion assumes that the number of consumers and their average expenditures for all income cells are known. Total expenditures can then be determined as the sum of expenditures in the cells. Klein proposed combining yearly income distribution data obtained from the tax authorities as a means of determining the number of consumers in income cells and a single consumer budget study to determine average expenditures in each income cell.

Then this idea is developed into the model of total consumer spending in this study. It is based on equation (3.3) in which individual consumption is separated into two components, an income term and a price term. Aggregate consumption is then shown to be an aggregate price term and the sum of individual income components. The individual income components are summed using the income distribution.

The sections below are brief because income distribution is only a necessary building block and is only indirectly related to the central question of this study. Therefore the theory is only reviewed in an attempt to limit the choice of density functions which can be used to model the distribution of income.

Literature Review

Theory. Sahota (1978), Aitchison and Brown (1957), and Champernowne (1953) survey the literature on the theories of personal income distribution. To summarize Sahota's findings, although income distribution has been well studied, there is no consensus theory which explains the observed distribution of incomes. All of the major theories — human capital, inheritance, and signalling — he concludes, have problems. All of the current theories reviewed by Sahota explain the observed distribution of income descriptively, but give few restrictions which shed light on any specific functional forms.

Some theories of income distribution result in specific functional forms. For example, the ability theory holds that individual characteristics such as intelligence determine earnings. If these qualities are distributed normally and affect earnings multiplicatively, then a lognormal distribution of earnings can result.

The lognormal distribution was developed by Aitchison and Brown (1957). In addition it can be derived as a result of the stochastic theory of income distribution. The log-normal distribution can be derived by assuming that the log of individual income is random and follows a first-order Markov process.

The assumptions required for both the stochastic and the ability theories are very restrictive and somewhat unbelievable. In addition, according to Sahota, these theories are not currently in favor. Therefore, the theories of income distribution cannot be used to select any specific functional forms and other criteria must be used.

Recent empirical studies. Recent empirical studies of income distribution have focused mainly on income inequality, either directly by measures such as the Lorenz curve and the Gini coefficient, or indirectly by fitting a continuous distribution to the observed data. The parameters of the fitted functions are then transformed into measures of inequality. Studies in this second group are useful to review because they deal with the estimation of income distribution functions. These studies can be used to choose a distribution function by providing information on the properties and fit of various functional forms.

For example, McDonald and Ransom (1979) estimate the parameters for four density functions—the log-normal, gamma, beta and Singh-Maddala—using U.S. family income data for 1960 and 1969 through 1975. They conclude that, on the basis of fit, the gamma performs better than the log-normal, but both of these are dominated by the three-parameter functions, the beta and the Singh-Maddala.

The Singh-Maddala function was developed by Singh and Maddala (1976) as a distribution function which would fit income data well. The function is based on the Pareto and is identical to it in the upper income tail.

McDonald and Ransom also present formulae for the population mean and variance as well as the Gini coefficient in terms of the parameters for the four functional forms. These will be used later to assess the properties of the various density functions.

In other empirical studies, models of income distribution have been linked to macro variables and also more complete economic systems. For example, Thurow (1970) fitted a beta density function to U.S. data for black and white households for the period 1944 to 1966. He then linked the estimated income distribution parameters to macro variables. For explanatory variables, Thurow decomposed aggregate nominal income per worker into four components:

$$\frac{\text{PIN}}{\text{LF}} = \frac{\text{GNP}}{\text{E}} \cdot \frac{\text{PI}}{\text{GNP}} \cdot \text{I} \cdot \frac{\text{E}}{\text{LF}} \tag{3.25}$$

where PIN is nominal personal income, PI is real personal income, LF is the labor force, E is employment, I is the price deflator, and GNP is nominal GNP. He then added government expenditures per household broken down into transfer payments and purchases. The estimated equation is then

$$\rho \text{ or } \sigma = A \cdot \left[\frac{\text{GNP}}{\text{E}}\right]^{b_0} \cdot \text{I}^{b_1} \cdot \left[\frac{\text{PI}}{\text{GNP}}\right]^{b_2} \cdot \left[\frac{\text{E}}{\text{LF}}\right]^{b_3} \cdot$$
$$\left[\frac{\text{TP}}{\text{H}}\right]^{b_4} \cdot \left[\frac{\text{GP}}{\text{H}}\right]^{b_5} \cdot e \tag{3.26}$$

where H are households, GP are government purchases, TP are transfers, and ρ, σ are parameters of beta density function.

Thurow's results for the estimated equations are difficult to interpret in terms of the effects of the macro variables on income distribution because of the opposite impacts of ρ and σ terms. Thurow shows that with the beta distribution, an increase in σ gives a higher median income and a smaller relative difference between lower and upper incomes. An increase in τ has opposite effects, reducing median income and increasing the relative differences in incomes. This is a problem because, in the estimated equations for σ and ρ, the coefficients for the same right-hand side variables have the same sign. Therefore a change in any of the explanatory variables which appears in both the σ and ρ equations will have off-setting effects on the median income and relative income differences. For example, real growth, characterized by GNP per employee, increases σ and ρ according to Thurow's equations for white households. The net effect is an increase in median income but no major change in the dispersion of income.

In a more recent article, Treyz, DuGuay, Chen and Williams (1981) fit a displaced lognormal density function to Massachusetts family income data for an eleven-year period. The income distribution parameters are then explained in three equations using regional variables. The model is used to test the effects of alternative tax policies on the distribution of family income.

The equations which link the income distribution to the regional economic variables indicate that increases in average wages increase average family income and reduce inequity by reducing the Gini coefficient. An increase in the unemployment rate displaces the distribution to lower income levels.

Functional forms. Based on theory, there is no clear-cut choice for a specific density function to model income distribution. The theories which Sahota considers to be at the forefront of research do not result in functional forms. This is not a criticism of the theories, but a statement that they are not helpful in this case.

Empirical studies offer more help. Studies which compare different functions in terms of fit offer some guidance. However, in choosing a density function, factors other than fit should be considered. Economic interpretation of the parameters and the properties of the function are examples. If these are taken into account, the difficulty in interpreting Thurow's results can be avoided. In addition, equations to explain the parameters are more easily specified.

This study uses the gamma density to model income distribution. The major reason for this choice is that the properties of this function can be interpreted in economic terms and these properties are desirable. This can be seen by writing several population statistics of the gamma in terms of its parameters. The gamma density has the form

$$f(Y) = \frac{1}{\Gamma(\alpha)}\beta^{\alpha}\ Y^{\alpha-1}\ e^{-Y/\beta} \tag{3.27}$$

where (α) is the gamma function.

The population statistics are

$$
\begin{aligned}
\text{mean} &= \alpha \cdot \beta \\
\text{variance} &= \alpha^2 \cdot \beta \\
\text{c.v.} &= \alpha.
\end{aligned}
\tag{3.28}
$$

These equations imply that the beta is a scale parameter and the alpha parameter is a measure of inequality. Alpha appears alone in the two measure of inequality, the c.v. and the Gini coefficient (see McDonald and Ransom (1979)). If it is fixed, then the relative distribution of income is fixed. Beta is a scale parameter because if all incomes change proportionally, then mean income will change by the same factor. If the relative distribution is fixed, then the mean income will change through β. Looked at in another way, changes in the relative distribution will only change α. In economic terms, the example where inflation raises all incomes by the same proportion and results in the same distribution of real income can be handled by the gamma. Shifts in relative income distribution can be seen by observing the alpha parameter.

Summary and Conclusion

This chapter develops a model of consumer demand which explicitly includes income distribution. The income distribution is included to maintain detail of individual expenditures by income class, which is usually lost in aggregation. Most aggregate consumption functions assume either a fixed income distribution or a single representative consumer with average income in the process of aggregating from microeconomic theory to macroeconomic consumption functions. Both of these assumptions prohibit the study of a redistribution of personal taxes by eliminating a variable distribution of disposable income.

The model aggregates from the micro to the macro level by simulating cross section expenditure equations over the entire income range. Expenditures at each income level are then summed to aggregate expenditures using the income distribution to determine the number of consumer units at each income level.

Two approaches to expenditures are developed. One is called the expenditure ratio method, and in it expenditures are computed at each income level using the observed ratio of expenditures to disposable income. The other approach uses cross section demand equations or Engel curves to determine expenditures by income level.

The estimation technique proposed requires two steps. First, the cross section relationships—the expenditure ratios and the Engel curves—are estimated from a single cross section sample. The resulting relationships are then simulated over the income distribution to produce synthetic variables, income components of expenditures for each year of the historical sample. The synthetic income variables are then used to estimate price terms using time series data.

The requirements for consistent aggregation and the estimation technique together impose restrictions on possible functional forms for the micro demand equations. The main restrictions are that the expenditure equation be normalized in the dependent variable and that the function be separable in the income and price terms. Separability of the income and price terms allows for the income component to be estimated using a single cross section sample and the price term be estimated in a second step using time series data.

The resulting model can be used to study a redistribution of taxes because it explicitly includes a variable distribution of disposable income. A change in tax rates for a single income class can be simulated because expenditures by income level are calculated. The estimation results are discussed in the next chapter.

4

Estimation of an Econometric Model of Consumer Demand

Introduction

Here the separate models of income distribution, taxes, and consumption derived and developed in earlier chapters are applied to U.S. data. The purpose of this chapter is to combine these three separate parts into a model of consumer demand which will incorporate personal federal taxes and be consistently aggregated. Two different approaches to consumer demand are developed and both can be used to study the effects of a restructuring of personal federal taxes on consumer expenditures and savings.

The two approaches to consumer demand differ in theoretical derivation and in the level of disaggregation of goods explained. The first is based on theory similar to the permanent income hypothesis and explains total expenditures. This method will be used to study the consumption savings decision directly. The second approach is based on several demand equations and explains demand for three categories of goods. In addition to an alternative method for studying savings, it can be used to examine the effects of changes in the distribution of disposable income on the allocation of consumer spending over different goods. Because the two approaches are similar in structure, they are included in a single model of consumer taxes and expenditures as competing alternatives.

Income Distribution

Data

Several sources of income distribution data are available for each year of the historical sample. The choice of the source used should be based on the intended use. In this study, income distribution data are used in modeling both tax collections and consumption. Different data sources are appropriate for each. For tax collections, the most desirable distribution is in terms of tax returns because, of course, taxes are based on income per tax return. However, to be consistent with the consumption part of the model, the distribution of income in terms of consumer units is more appropriate. These two distributions are not necessarily the same because it is possible for one consumer unit to have more than one tax return. An example is the case of a teenager who holds a part-time job and files a tax return but is still part of the family spending unit.

The definition of a tax return, necessary to understand the distribution of income by tax returns, is simple. A tax return is a document filed with the tax authority (IRS) on which taxes owed are based. Tax returns are filed by all income recipients depending on marital status. The actual requirements of who must file a tax return are complicated and have changed over the years. Basically, any individual or married couple with an income above a minimum must file a tax return. Therefore the distribution of income by tax return gives the number of returns at any given level of income.

The term "consumer unit", however, is an abstract concept which is useful in applying consumer theory to observed data. Consumer theory is based on the assumption that an individual chooses the set of most preferred goods, subject to a budget constraint. However, it is unrealistic to assume that each member of the population makes all of his or her own consumption decisions. The extreme example, of course, is an infant who is cared for by its parents. As a solution, groups of individuals can be considered to make consumption decisions as one entity, a consumer unit. Alternatively, one member makes decisions for the group. The underlying assumption is that the consumer unit can order its preferences in the same way as individuals are assumed to do.

For example, the 1972 Consumer Expenditure Survey defines a consumer unit as "(1) a group of two persons or more, usually living together, who pool their income and draw from a common fund for their major items of expense, or (2) a person living alone or sharing a household with others, or a roomer . . . who is financially independent" (p. 126). This definition, on which the consumption data used later are based, is consistent with the idea that consumption decisions are made by families or by individuals living alone.

There are two major possibilities for income distribution data consistent with the notion of consumer units and which are available for each year of the historical sample. Data available are distributions by households or by families and unrelated individuals. The closest match to the definition of consumer unit used in the 1972 Consumer Expenditure Survey is the combination of families and unrelated individuals. (U.S. Bureau of the Census, 1960–1981. Data for households are available beginning in 1967. Data for families and also for unrelated individuals begin in 1947.) According to the census definition, a family is a group of two or more persons living together. This definition is similar to the first condition of a consumer unit used in the consumption data. An unrelated individual is defined as a single person not living with relatives. This definition is similar to the second condition for a consumer unit. Therefore the sum of families and unrelated individuals defined by the census closely matches the definition of consumer units used by the Bureau of Labor Statistics.

The census definition of a household is not as close a match to the consumption data because it includes independent persons such as a boarder living with a family as a member of the household.

Because the definition of families and unrelated individuals is closer to the definition of a consumer unit used in collecting the consumption data, we focus on the distributions of income for U.S. families and also unrelated individuals. The choice gives a complete accounting of consumer units.

From the point of view of modeling consumer expenditures, using two income distributions has the advantage that expenditures can be estimated for two demographic groups, families and unrelated individuals. This approach could be an advantage because the two groups might have different spending patterns. For example, each group has a different number of members. By definition, unrelated individuals are single persons, while families have more than one member.

However, this demographic concept is not easily applied in this study because of the problem matching the tax and consumption data. The tax distribution data on which the tax rates are based are published by type of return, not household status. To separate consumer units by family status would also require tax rates by family status. To simplify this mismatch problem, this study combines families and unrelated individuals into the general category, consumer units, and tax rates are an average of all types of returns. In future work with more tax detail, different types of consumer units could be identified.

The income distributions for both families and unrelated individuals are estimated separately in an attempt to better fit the data. They are then combined into one distribution of consumer unit income.

The income distribution data available are given in histogram form which gives the percentage of all families (unrelated individuals) with income falling within the 11 reported income cells. (U.S. Bureau of the Census, 1980. This source is chosen because it gives constant dollar distributions for all of the years of history used in fixed income classes.) The histograms used are in real terms in that the cells are given in constant 1980 dollars.

Estimation Techniques

As discussed in chapter 3, the gamma distribution was chosen to model the distribution of income because its parameters can be interpreted in economic terms. Estimating the parameters of a gamma density function is not straightforward because the function is nonlinear in the parameters. Therefore a nonlinear estimation method is necessary.

Techniques for estimating the parameters of continuous density functions using grouped data are reviewed in McDonald and Ransom (1979), and their results are directly applicable to the estimation of the gamma. The basic approach is to specify an objective function and search for the parameter values which give the extreme value of the objective function. McDonald and Ransom give three different objective function methods. They are (1) The method of scoring estimators defines those which maximize

$$n! \left(\frac{p_i \cdot n_i}{n_i!} \right) \tag{4.1}$$

where $p_i = \sum_{I_i} f(y)dy$,

n_i is the actual fraction in cell i, and
I_i is income range for cell i_a;

(2) Pearson minimum chi-square estimators define those which minimize

$$n \cdot \sum_i (n_i - p_i)^2 / p_i. \tag{4.2}$$

(3) Least squares estimators minimize

$$\sum_i (n_i - p_i)^2. \tag{4.3}$$

McDonald and Ransom report that the method of scoring and minimum chi-squares are efficient estimators. An estimator is defined to be efficient if the variance of the estimator is equal to the Cramer-Rao lower bound. For a discussion of efficient estimators and the Cramer-Rao lower bound for the variance of unbiased estimators, see Mood, Graybill, and Boes (1974). The method of scoring is asymptotically efficient according to McDonald and Ransom because it can be considered a maximum likelihood estimator. The chi-square estimator is also efficient because it is asymptotically equivalent to the scoring estimators.

The minimum chi-square technique has the added advantage that it can be interpreted as a weighted least squares estimator where each observation is weighted by n/p_i, which gives the smaller intervals — the lower and upper tails — more weight.

In searching for the optimal parameters, the actual fraction of the population in each income cell is taken from the data. The predicted values are computed by approximating the gamma density function over each income interval. The approximation is done by the method of trapezoids and breaks each income interval into 20 subintervals. For the top bracket which is open ended, the density function is evaluated up to about 10 times the mean income. At that income level, the value of the density function equals zero, and further calculations would not change the results.

Estimation Results

The gamma distribution was fitted to U.S. family as well as unrelated individual income distributions for the sample period 1960–1980. The two parameters of the gamma distribution were estimated by grid search, which yielded the minimum value for the chi-square statistic as described above.

The estimated parameters for both distributions are shown in table 4.1. For families, the results can be said to be reasonable in that they are similar to those in previous studies of the gamma distribution, such as Salem and Mount (1974) and also McDonald and Ransom (1979). Salem and Mount fit the gamma to U.S. family data for 1960–1969 and McDonald and Ransom for 1960 and 1969–1975. The results in this study are slightly different, probably because different data were used.

As was discussed in chapter 3, the beta parameter is a scale term which shifts the distribution with no impact on skewness. Changes in the alpha parameter indicate changes in skewness with an increase in alpha indicating less inequality. The results in table 4.1 indicate that family and also unrelated individual income distributions are becoming less unequal.

This result may be due to the collector effect which questions intertemporal comparisons of income distributions. The collector effect is the problem of income distributions seeming to become more heavily weighted in the upper income levels over time when in fact the underlying distribution is only being rescaled by inflation. The problem occurs when the income distribution data are reported in the same income classes over a long period. (For details on the collector effect see Petersen (1979).)

Estimated changes in inequality over time might be due to the collector effect. However, this problem is minimized because the income distribution data used are reported in income intervals scaled for inflation.

The actual and predicted percentages of families and also unrelated individuals in each income cell are compared for the historical sample

Table 4.1. Estimated Parameters for Gamma Income Distribution. Unrelated Individuals

Date	Alpha	Beta
1960	1.00	6.28
1961	1.00	6.54
1962	1.00	4.22
1963	1.00	6.72
1964	1.00	7.32
1965	1.00	7.42
1966	1.04	7.33
1967	1.02	7.67
1968	1.17	7.28
1969	1.19	7.28
1970	1.26	7.06
1971	1.33	6.72
1972	1.37	6.78
1973	1.44	6.77
1974	1.55	4.71
1975	1.59	6.01
1976	1.56	6.36
1977	1.65	6.24
1978	1.62	6.61
1979	1.64	6.55
1980	1.64	6.55

Table 4.1. (Continued) Estimated Parameters for Gamma Income Distribution. Families

Date	Alpha	Beta
1960	2.19	7.14
1961	2.11	7.62
1962	2.22	7.35
1963	2.22	7.60
1964	2.25	7.75
1965	2.29	7.86
1966	2.44	7.81
1967	2.40	8.13
1968	2.16	8.37
1969	2.44	8.83
1970	2.36	9.17
1971	2.37	9.13
1972	2.34	9.72
1973	2.39	9.72
1974	2.29	9.95
1975	2.33	9.60
1976	2.33	9.90
1977	2.26	10.44
1978	2.26	10.73
1979	2.16	11.47
1980	2.14	11.16

1960–1980 in the appendix. In general, the fits are acceptable. However there are some relatively large errors in the small income cells. Later, errors in small cells will cause errors in taxes and expenditures.

Personal Federal Taxes

Rates

Personal federal tax collections are based on the income distributions estimated above, and the effective tax rates computed for each historical sample year. The method of computing the effective tax table is discussed in chapter 3. To review, average tax rates for 20 income brackets are computed as the ratio of federal taxes paid to the reported adjusted gross income in each of the 20 brackets. The data are taken from the IRS publication, *Statistics of Income*, for the years 1960 through 1978. Because the reported income brackets change, the model tax brackets change from year to year. In most years, there are more than 20 brackets reported and therefore some of the brackets are aggregated together. From these average rates, the implied marginal rates are computed. The marginal rates are used in the model to make it more like the actual tax law. As an example, the effective tax rates for 1978, the last year for which data were available when the calculations were made, are shown in table 4.2.

As discussed in chapter 3, the effective rates are lower than the statutory rates. The major reason for this is that the reduction in taxes due to deductions and exemptions is absorbed in the effective tax rates. In addition, the effective tax rates are the average of tax rates for the different rates by marital status and therefore are not easily compared with the published tax schedules.

Distribution of Tax Base Income

As mentioned above, tax rates are based on taxes and income by tax return by income level. Therefore the tax rates implicitly include the distribution of tax return (adjusted gross) income. If these rates were applied to the exact distribution of tax return income, taxes by bracket and the aggregate would be predicted perfectly. However, this study uses the distribution of consumer unit income which in general has a lower density at low income levels than the distribution of tax return income. The reason for this is that one consumer unit can have more than one tax return and this can lower the tax liability of the consumer unit. Therefore, using the distribution of income by consumer units which has more weight in the higher income levels can result in overcollections.

Table 4.2.   Effective Tax Rates — 1978

| Adjusted Gross Income (Thousands of Dollars) | | | Tax Rate (Percent) | |
Above	but	Below	Marginal	Average
0		2	0.068	0.137
2		4	0.784	0.569
4		6	7.438	3.336
6		7	10.449	4.978
7		8	12.928	6.030
8		9	15.580	7.160
9		10	13.992	7.880
10		11	14.854	8.544
11		12	14.758	9.084
12		13	17.485	9.756
13		14	15.915	10.213
14		15	17.354	10.705
15		20	16.885	11.764
20		25	18.410	13.241
25		30	22.554	14.934
30		50	24.101	17.799
50		100	33.141	24.959
100		200	42.070	33.515
200		500	44.671	39.890
	Over 500		48.940	44.717

The actual and predicted distributions of tax return income are compared for one sample year, 1978, in table 4.3. The actual and predicted distributions could be compared for any historical year. Only one is shown because the tax-bracket definitions change over the years and therefore tables are time-consuming to produce. The actual distribution data are scaled so that both sum to the same aggregate income. The comparisons show that the model underpredicts tax return income in the lower- to middle-income range and overpredicts at higher incomes. This can result in overpredicted aggregate collections.

As expected, this pattern is repeated when comparing actual and predicted collections by income bracket. However, the underprediction in the low and very high brackets is offset by overpredictions in the middle and upper brackets.

Aggregate Results

Total estimated tax collections are compared to the actual collections in table 4.4. Over the sample the results are good although with small errors

Table 4.3.   Distribution of Tax Return Income — 1978

Tax Bracket (Thousands of Dollars)		Share of Aggregate Income		
		Actual	Predicted	Difference
0	2	0.72	0.20	0.52
2	4	2.11	0.95	1.15
4	6	3.23	1.78	1.45
6	7	2.18	1.30	0.88
7	8	2.20	1.41	0.80
8	9	2.39	1.71	0.68
9	10	2.34	1.76	0.58
10	11	2.53	2.05	0.48
11	12	2.59	1.87	0.72
12	13	2.78	2.30	0.48
13	14	2.75	2.40	0.35
14	15	2.83	2.48	0.35
15	20	15.18	12.12	3.06
20	25	14.58	12.60	1.98
25	30	11.21	11.02	0.19
30	50	18.24	28.49	-10.25
50	100	7.35	15.13	-7.78
100	200	2.86	0.42	2.45
200	500	1.28	0	1.28
500	1000	0.65	0	0.65

each year. However, except for 1972, the estimated taxes always exceed the actual, which indicates a bias problem. The largest percentage error is an underprediction and occurs in 1975, a recession year. The only overprediction is in 1972, a high growth year.

After explaining the largest errors, the question of bias needs to be addressed. The most likely cause is that the distribution of income used is inconsistent with the tax rates. As mentioned above, tax rates are based on taxes and income by tax return but the income distribution is in terms of consumer units. Aggregate collections will be overpredicted if the actual tax rates for a consumer unit at a given income level are lower than the tax rate for a tax return at the same income level. This is possible because one consumer unit can have more than one tax return. By dividing income into tax returns for its members, a consumer unit can reduce its effective tax rate.

As a result of this mismatch in the income distribution and tax rates, the predictions of aggregate tax collections are biased upward. To account for this in estimation and simulation of the expenditure equations, all tax rates have been multiplied by a fixed percentage (identical for each income

Table 4.4.   Actual vs. Estimated Aggregate Personal Federal Taxes

Date	Actual	Predicted	Difference	% Difference
1960	43.644	45.080	-1.436	-3.291
1961	44.704	47.254	-2.550	-5.704
1962	48.635	51.300	-2.665	-5.480
1963	51.483	53.945	-2.462	-4.782
1964	48.626	53.325	-4.699	-9.664
1965	53.947	55.819	-1.872	-3.471
1966	61.696	63.845	-2.149	-3.483
1967	67.475	69.969	-2.494	-3.696
1968	79.661	83.946	-4.285	-5.379
1969	95.113	96.941	-1.828	-1.922
1970	92.611	96.315	-3.704	-4.000
1971	90.305	96.453	-6.148	-6.808
1972	108.209	100.845	7.364	6.805
1973	114.702	120.388	-5.686	-4.958
1974	131.260	135.982	-4.722	-3.598
1975	125.830	138.446	-12.616	-10.026
1976	147.273	154.793	-7.520	-5.106
1977	170.052	180.474	-10.422	-6.128
1978	194.921	213.223	-18.302	-9.389

bracket but different each year). The percentage is calculated for each year so that the model predicts history exactly. The correction amounts to roughly a 5 percent reduction in each year, except for 1972 when the rates were increased slightly.

Alternative approaches were considered. For example, no adjustment to the rates was tried with very little change in estimation results for expenditures. In estimation, which is discussed in the next section, only the intercept term changed by any noticeable amount. Because only the intercept term was changed, simulation results should not be affected.

Consumption Equations

The consumption function for both the expenditure ratio and demand equation approaches are estimated in two steps. First, the microeconomic individual consumer relationships are estimated from cross section data. These equations are then simulated over the distribution of disposable income to produce the income components of consumption for each year of the historical sample. The second step is to estimate the time series effects — relative price effects, in this case — using aggregate consumption data, the constructed income components, and prices. This two-stage method allows consistent aggregation of the micro equations.

To review, the general form of the consumption function is

$$X_i = g(YD_i) + h(P) \tag{4.4}$$

where X_i is the demand for good X by consumer i, YD_i is the disposable income of consumer i, and P is the price of good X relative to other consumer good prices. This general form gives individual consumer unit expenditures as functions of the consumer unit's income and relative prices. Demographic information specific to the consumer unit, such as size or age of head, has not been included. To maintain consistent aggregation by simulating individual consumer units over the population and to include specific demographic information would require joint distributions of income and the demographic variables. Such a generalization would be useful, but is beyond the scope of this study.

The $g(\cdot)$ term is estimated from cross section data because, assuming prices are constant over a budget study, the $h(\cdot)$ term can be dropped.

Given the $g(\cdot)$ function, the price component can be estimated. First the price term is isolated:

$$X_i - g(YD_i) = h(P). \tag{4.5}$$

Summing over individuals,

$$\sum_i X_i - \sum_i g\ (YD_i) = \sum_i h(P), \tag{4.6}$$

$$X - \sum g\ (YD_i)\ /\ N = h(P). \tag{4.7}$$

The $g(\cdot)$ term represents the simulation of the $g(\cdot)$ function over the distribution of disposable income. It includes the tax rates which have not been written out explicitly for the sake of simplicity. Equation (4.7) can be used to estimate the price effect, $h(\cdot)$.

The procedure is used for both the expenditure ratio and demand equation models. Each is presented separately because of slight modifications necessary.

Expenditure Ratio Method

The expenditure ratio method in chapter 3 gives the individual consumer unit's consumption function as

$$C_i = b_i\ (YD_i, r)\cdot YD_i \tag{4.8}$$

where r is the after-tax rate of return, and $b_i(\cdot)$ is the ratio of expenditures to disposable income for consumer i. This equation cannot be estimated by combining a single cross-section sample with aggregate time series data as described above because the income term which corresponds to the general $g(\cdot)$ in equation (4.5) depends on the time series, the after-tax rate of return which varies over the income range and over time.

As an alternative, the equation can be simplified to

$$C_i = b(YD_i) \cdot YD_i + h(r) \qquad (4.9)$$

where the income component is

$$C_i^* = b(YD_i) \cdot YD_i \qquad (4.10)$$

when C_i^* is the income component of expenditures for consumer i. This is a simplification because the after tax-rate of return has been removed from the income component function. In addition, it is a simplification because the after-tax rate of return should use the individual consumer unit's marginal tax rate, where in this case only an aggregate average can be used. This implies that the aggregation of the interest rate term is not consistent.

The equation can be estimated by the above method and have an income term which is consistently aggregated.

The income coefficient can be estimated from cross section data as the ratio of total consumption to disposable income for each income class. However, this would result in a step function with jumps in the levels of the income term as the income brackets change. As an alternative, this study interpolates the income terms between the income brackets. This produces a step function with jumps in the slope of the function, but not in the level. The income terms are determined by the equation

$$b(YD_i) = b^{I-1} - \frac{(b^I - b^{I-1})}{(BKT^I - BKT^{I-1})} \cdot (YD_i - BKT^{I-1}) \qquad (4.11)$$

where BKT^I is the upper limit income cell I when $BKT^{I-1} < YD_i < BKT^I$.

The expenditure ratios for the twelve income classes are shown in table 4.5. The table shows that for incomes up to \$5,000, expenditures exceed disposable income. Assuming that each income cell is a consumer unit, this is difficult to accept because expenditures exceeding disposable income is a violation of the consumer unit's budget constraint. Some possible explanations, such as changes in the value of financial assets which would imply wealth rather than income as the binding constraint, cannot account for the excess expenditures. Therefore, it is likely that the problem is in the data.

As a result, two alternatives are considered. First, the data are used

Table 4.5.   Expenditure Income Ratios —
1972 Consumer Expenditure Survey

| Brackets | | Ratio |
(Thousands of 1972 Dollars)		
0.00	3.00	1.95
3.00	4.00	1.24
4.00	5.00	1.11
5.00	6.00	1.05
6.00	7.00	1.01
7.00	8.00	0.96
8.00	10.00	0.91
10.00	12.00	0.86
12.00	15.00	0.81
15.00	20.00	0.75
20.00	25.00	0.70
25.00	and above	0.56

exactly as in table 4.5. This implies marginal propensities to consume greater than 1.0 at low incomes with these consumers violating their budget constraints. As an alternative, the data are assumed to be incorrect and the true expenditure ratios are assumed to be less than 1.0. For incomes below $5,000, the ratio is assumed to be 0.986, the first observed value less than 1.0.

These two alternatives are both tested and the results are discussed below. To summarize, there are large differences in the cross section results in the first few income classes where the expenditure ratios were changed, but because only a small percentage of total expenditures comes from these classes, the aggregate results are not affected.

Time Series Effects

Simulating equation (4.10) over the distribution of disposable income for the historical sample produces the income component of aggregate consumption. The difference between actual consumption and this income component can then be attributed to price effects. This residual in per-consumer-unit terms is calculated as

$$\text{Residual} = [C - \sum_{i=1}^{n} b(YD_i) \cdot YD_i]/n \qquad (4.12)$$

Table 4.6. Per Capita Price Component
of Total Expenditures —
Expenditure Ratio Method

1960	0.15282
1961	0.11886
1962	0.23915
1963	0.32467
1964	0.36885
1965	0.38013
1966	0.52984
1967	0.45268
1968	0.63749
1969	0.70467
1970	0.49032
1971	0.50456
1972	0.57916
1973	0.61121
1974	0.44817
1975	0.39435
1976	0.58962
1977	0.79614
1978	0.88835
1979	0.84449
1980	0.72368
1981	0.70554

where C is the aggregate consumption. The result is shown in table 4.6.

Examination of table 4.6 shows that there is a positive trend in aggregate price component of consumption which is large and could be caused by factors other than changes in interest rates. Regressing first stage the consumption residual on a time trend shows that 37 percent of the variation is explained by a time trend alone. This result can be explained in many ways, such as a shift in the expenditure shares b_i, or an unmeasured shift in the income distribution. In any case, the time trend effect is small, adding about $10 per year to each consumer unit's consumption. Even in the lowest income class, this amounts to less than one percent of consumption.

Several different definitions of the after-tax rate of return were tried in the second step of estimation. All were tried with and without the time trend variable. The definitions varied in the base interest rate, and in the treatment of inflation and taxes. Most failed to produce statistically significant coefficients either positive or negative in sign. This finding is not surprising because consumer theory does not restrict the sign of this term. Recall that a change in the after-tax real rate of return will increase the budget set of a net saver and decrease it for a net dissaver and for both it will increase the price of current consumption relative to future consumption. Therefore, the direction of a change in consumption due to interest rates cannot be determined in the aggregate.

However, one definition, given below, does result in small but statistically significant negative coefficients using various specifications which used different lag patterns. Because this definition is robust in the sense that different specifications produce similar results, it is used in the final model.

Estimation Results

The final estimated equation is shown in figure 4.1. The first-degree Almon lag was chosen because it imposed the à priori belief of declining effects of a change in interest rates over time and still yielded reasonable results.

The after-tax rate of return is defined as

$$r = FRMCS \cdot (1 - AR) - PDOT \tag{4.13}$$

where *FRMCS* is the long term bond rate, *AR* is the average aggregate tax rate, and *PDOT* is inflation. The nominal interest rate is the rate of return on long term bonds discounted by the average aggregate tax rate. The rate is made "real" by subtracting current inflation.

The test statistics reported with the estimated equation do not reflect the fit of estimated aggregate consumption because the dependent variable in the regression is the residual price component term. The fit for aggregate consumption is reported below.

This equation can be solved for the individual consumer unit consumption function by combining the results of the two stages of estimation. The individual function is

$$C_i = 0.0096 \cdot t + b_i \, YD_i - 0.0079 \cdot r \tag{4.14}$$

$$-0.0236 \cdot r_{-1} - 0.0315 \cdot r_{-2}$$

where C_i are individual expenditures, 1972 dollars and t is the time trend.

The properties of the individual consumer unit are easy to show. At zero income and mean values for the time trend and interest rate variables, consumption is slightly positive. The time trend alone adds $10 (in 1972 dollars) to consumption each year. The long-run effect of a one percentage

Figure 4.1.   Time Series Estimated Equation—Expenditure Ratio Approach

Z.CE =   + 0.0096 DUMTIME 46
               (8.3756)

          – 0.0079 LONGRR   –   0.0157 LONGRR(-1)   –   0.0236 LONGRR(-2)
               (–1.9679)   (–1.9679)   (–1.9679)

          – 0.0315 LONGRR(-3)
               (–1.9679)

         R-SQUARED(CORR.): 0.410   SEE: 0.16247   DW: 0.61

         PERIOD OF FIT: 1960   1981

         F(2,20):   7.796

         WHERE:

                    Z.CE = TOTAL AGGREGATE EXPENDITURES - YP.CE
                    YP.CE = INCOME COMPONENT OF TOTAL EXPENDITURES
                              COMPUTED USING INCOME DISTRIBUTION
                    LONGRR = FRMCS * (1.0 – TXCPF$ / AGI$) – PDOT
                    FRMCS = INTEREST RATE, LONG TERM BONDS
                    TXCPF$ = TOTAL PERSONAL FEDERAL TAX COLLECTIONS
                    AGI$ = ADJUSTED GROSS INCOME
                    PDOT = PERCENT CHANGE, CONSUMER PRICE DEFLATOR

point increase in the after-tax real rate of return is a decrease in consumption of $195 (in 1972 dollars). The marginal propensity to consume depends on the level of disposable income.

The major problem with this equation is that the time series terms affect consumption independent of the level of income or consumption. Thus a change in interest rates will change the consumption of all consumer units by the same amount. The poorest individual will have the same level of response as the richest. This is clearly unreasonable, but given the constraints on functional forms imposed by consistent aggregation, there is no tractable solution using the current estimation method.

Aggregate consumption is the sum of the expenditures of all consumer units. Disposable income at each level of income is personal income less federal taxes, a fixed rate state and local government tax and contributions to social insurance based on the actual law.

The estimated aggregate consumption is shown in table 4.7. The model fits well over the sample period with a root mean square error of 1.6. The largest single period relative errors are overpredictions and occur in 1960 and 1961, periods of slow economic growth. The model also overpredicts total expenditures in 1974, when actual real consumer expenditures fell.

Table 4.7.   Actual vs. Predicted Aggregate Real Consumer Expenditures

Date	Actual	Predicted	Difference	% Difference
1960	452.000	460.805	−8.805	−1.948
1961	461.400	470.944	−9.544	−2.069
1962	482.000	485.698	−3.698	−0.767
1963	500.500	502.518	−2.018	−0.403
1964	528.000	532.196	−4.196	−0.795
1965	557.500	560.545	−3.045	−0.546
1966	585.700	584.064	1.636	0.279
1967	602.700	605.904	−3.204	−0.532
1968	634.400	630.401	3.999	0.630
1969	657.900	648.499	9.401	1.429
1970	672.100	674.882	−2.782	−0.414
1971	696.800	698.985	−2.185	−0.314
1972	737.100	723.098	14.001	1.900
1973	768.500	767.369	1.131	0.147
1974	763.600	779.936	−16.336	−2.139
1975	780.200	802.285	−22.086	−2.831
1976	823.100	824.898	−1.798	−0.218
1977	864.354	851.683	12.671	1.466
1978	903.202	888.418	14.783	1.637
1979	927.599	911.927	15.672	1.689
1980	930.488	923.777	6.711	0.721
1981	947.656	934.811	12.844	1.355

This drop was not picked up by the model. On the other hand, 1972, a high growth year, did not result in underprediction. Therefore, a systematic error such as is found in the tax collection mechanism is not a likely problem.

The income response properties of the aggregate results depend on the income distribution and therefore cannot be studied analytically in any detail. Therefore discussion of these responses follows in chapter 5.

The model also produces cross section results which are reported in real terms in twelve income intervals or cells. These results cannot be directly compared with history because detailed cross section expenditure data are not available over time. However, the model results can be compared with the 1972 Consumer Expenditure Survey in share of aggregate form.

To summarize the cross section expenditure fit which is discussed in detail below: although there are some large percentage errors in the lower income intervals, these errors have little impact on the aggregate results because only a small percentage of the aggregate originates at these income levels. There is also a large percentage error in the highest interval, but the error declines when the top four cells are added together.

Demand Equation Method

This section presents the estimation of the demand equation approach to consumer spending. In chapter 3 it was shown that total consumer demand can be estimated by summing the demands for specific goods. Savings is determined as a residual category. To apply this idea, consumer demand is broken down into three categories: durables, nondurables, and services. Although many disaggregation schemes are possible, disaggregation by type of good allows a small number of categories to be tested, and at the same time allows the categories to sum to total expenditures. The other major basis of aggregation, by use of good, would require at least seven categories to be studied. Because disaggregation of consumer goods is not the focus of this study, the simpler scheme is used.

Cross Section Demand Equations

The demand equation model developed in chapter 3 gives consumer unit i's demand for good x as

$$X_i = a + b \cdot \ln YD_i + c \cdot P. \tag{4.15}$$

This equation can be estimated by the two steps outlined earlier in this chapter. The income component of demand is estimated from the cross section sample and the estimated equations are of the form

$$X_i = a + b \cdot \ln YD_i. \tag{4.16}$$

This equation is a semilog Engel curve and the estimation results are displayed below. Recall that for aggregation by simulation, the underlying micro equation must be linear in the dependent variable and nonlinear in the independent variables. (A linear equation would give no distributional effects and would not follow observed declining marginal propensities to consume in cross section data.) Specifications other than semilog were tried, but did not produce reasonable results. For example, a quadratic equation gave negative expenditures at high incomes.

Estimation using cross section data presents the possibility of heteroscedastic errors which causes least squares estimators not to be the most efficient unbiased estimators possible. According to Johnston (1972), it is likely that the variance of the residual terms of demand equations estimated using cross section data are heteroscedastic because the variance increases with income. He suggests two models of disturbance. In the first, disturbances increase proportionally with income, and in the second disturbances increase proportionally with the square of income. Johnston then shows that a simple weighting of the observations gives a generalized least squares estimator which is unbiased and efficient.

Regressions using both weighting schemes were tried for all three categories of expenditures and, with one exception, failed to produce statistically significant coefficients. This failure is likely due to the small sample size. Therefore the ordinary least squares estimates are used and the estimated equations are shown in figure 4.2.

Figure 4.2.   Cross Section Expenditure Income Estimated Equations

DURABLE GOODS

CED.CEX = −0.7217 + 0.9902 LOG(YPD.CEX)
         (−3.3342)   (9.8696)

R-SQUARED(CORR.): 0.898   SEE: 0.26459

NONDURABLE GOODS

CEN.CEX = −0.4678 + 1.7427 LOG(YPD.CEX)
         (−1.4752)   (11.8553)

R-SQUARED(CORR.): 0.927   SEE: 0.38766

SERVICES

CES.CEX = −0.5935 + 2.0888 LOG(YPD.CEX)
         (−1.0389)   (7.8873)

R-SQUARED(CORR.): 0.848   SEE: 0.69840

WHERE:
        CED.CEX = DURABLE EXPENDITURES
        CEN.CEX = NONDURABLE EXPENDITURES
        CES.CEX = SERVICES EXPENDITURES
        YPD.CEX = DISPOSABLE INCOME

Estimation Results

Given the cross section equations, the income components of demand over the historical sample can be calculated by evaluating the cross section equations over the distribution of disposable income. As with the expenditure ratio method, per-consumer-unit residual price component can be calculated as

$$(X - \sum_{i=1}^{n} (a + b \cdot \ln YD_i)) / n - c \cdot P \qquad (4.17)$$

The results are shown in table 4.8. These results indicate that there is likely a time trend effect which is due to more than price changes in the expenditures net of income for these three categories. Regressions using a time trend variable alone explain 60 percent of the variation in the nondurables category and over 80 percent in the durables and services categories. A possible explanation is that the intercept terms in the underlying demand equations are shifting over time, which implies that expenditures at zero income are rising over time. Another explanation would be an income effect which is not captured by the income distribution term. In either case the demand equation becomes

$$X_i = a(t) + b \cdot \ln (YD_i) + c \cdot P \qquad (4.18)$$

Table 4.8.   Per Capita Price Components of
Expenditures — Demand Equation Approach

Date	Durables	Nondurables	Services
1960	−0.28730	0.79448	−0.32531E−01
1961	−0.35036	0.79294	0.34075E−01
1962	−0.27390	0.83530	0.11843
1963	−0.24659	0.79178	0.13311
1964	−0.22373	0.83210	0.18552
1965	−0.15917	0.85150	0.19807
1966	−0.12186	0.91294	0.23542
1967	−0.15391	0.86354	0.30304
1968	−0.70174E−01	0.88776	0.33142
1969	−0.57954E−01	0.87856	0.41540
1970	−0.15200	0.83988	0.42641
1971	−0.62699E−01	0.80106	0.45987
1972	0.54765E−01	0.80405	0.49373
1973	0.12834	0.74878	0.51020
1974	−0.12339E−01	0.60456	0.54680
1975	−0.43379E−01	0.58341	0.59774
1976	0.83726E−01	0.62752	0.64100
1977	0.17798	0.65545	0.73492
1978	0.22204	0.63604	0.78564
1979	0.18354	0.64405	0.85423
1980	0.38878E−01	0.59865	0.88020
1981	0.40337E−01	0.59104	0.86592

where $a(t)$ is a function of time. If the intercept term is a linear function of time, then the demand equation can be rewritten

$$X_i = a_0 + a_1 \cdot t + b \cdot \ln YD_i + c \cdot P. \tag{4.19}$$

Isolating the time series component, which now includes a time trend, and summing over the income distribution gives

$$\sum_{i=1}^{n} (X_i - a_0 - b \cdot \ln YD_i) / n = a_i \cdot t + c \cdot P \tag{4.20}$$

or

$$(X - \sum_{i=1}^{n} (a_0 + b \cdot \ln YD_i)) / n = a_i \cdot t + c \cdot P. \tag{4.21}$$

The left-hand side of equation (4.21) is aggregate spending on good x net of the income effect and is used in the second step estimation of the time trend and price effects. The time series regression becomes

$$Z_X = a_1 \cdot t + c \cdot P_X \tag{4.22}$$

where Z_X is the per capita demand for good x net of income component.

The regression results are displayed in figure 4.3. In the case of durables, the time trend was dropped because its coefficient could not be distinguished from zero. The test statistics displayed refer to the estimated equations and, because the dependent variables are the residual time trend components, do not indicate how well aggregate expenditures are explained.

The individual consumer unit demand equations for each of the three categories have the same properties. An increase in disposable income results in an increase in expenditures. However, because of the functional form imposed by exact aggregation and the two stage estimation method used, the marginal propensities to spend in all categories fall as income rises. Therefore, the marginal propensity to save rises as individual incomes rise.

An increase in the relative price of a good causes real expenditures to fall. However, this price effect is a problem in that a given change will change the expenditures of all consumers by the same level amount. This is also a result of the functional form.

The equations for the three categories are different because of the different estimated coefficients. For example, a consumer unit's expenditures on durables grows approximately $10 per year due to the time trend while expenditures on services grow by about $51 per year. The relative

Figure 4.3. Time Series Estimated Equations — Demand Equation Approach

DURABLE GOODS

Z.CED = 0.0104 DUMTIME46 – 0.3826 RPDCED – 0.2551 RPDCED(–1) – 0.1275 RPDCED(–2)
      (8.72)   (–9.04)   (–9.04)   (–9.04)

R-SQUARED(CORR.): 0.783   SEE: 0.76222e–01   DW:1.16
PERIOD OF FIT: 1960 1981   F(2,20): 38.327

WHERE:
  Z.CED = AGGREGATE DURABLE EXPENDITURES LESS INCOME COMPONENT
           COMPUTED USING INCOME DISTRIBUTION
  RPDCED = PRICE OF DURABLE GOODS RELATIVE TO ALL CONSUMER GOODS

NONDURABLE GOODS

Z.CEN = 6.6491 – 2.8913 RPDCEN – 1.9276 RPDCEN(–1) – 0.9638 RPDCEN(–2)
      (–13.4) (–11.8)   (–11.8)   (–11.8)

R-SQUARED(CORR.): 0.869   SEE: 0.76222e–01   DW: 0.96
PERIOD OF FIT: 1960 1981   F(2,20): 140.47

WHERE:
  Z.CEN = AGGREGATE NONDURABLE EXPENDITURES LESS INCOME COMPONENT
           COMPUTED USING INCOME DISTRIBUTION
  RPDCED = PRICE OF NONDURABLE GOODS RELATIVE TO ALL CONSUMER GOODS

SERVICES

Z.CES = 0.0514 DUMTIME46 – 1.6320 RPDCES – 1.0880 RPDCES(–1) – 0.5440 RPDCES(–2)
      (–31.6)   (–27.8)   (–27.8)   (–27.8)

R-SQUARED(CORR.): 0.981   SEE: 0.38505E–01   DW: 0.89
PERIOD OF FIT: 1960 1981   F(2,20): 563.40

WHERE:
  Z.CES = AGGREGATE SERVICE EXPENDITURES LESS INCOME COMPONENT COMPUTED
          USING INCOME DISTRIBUTION
  RPDCES = PRICE OF SERVICES RELATIVE TO ALL CONSUMER GOODS

price effects are also different. Durables are the least sensitive while nondurables are the most.

As with total expenditures, the cross section demand category results cannot be compared with actual data because of data problems. However, the results for the twelve income classes can be compared with the 1972 Consumer Expenditure Survey in share of aggregate form.

To summarize, the results of the cross section comparison for the three categories of demand are similar to those for total expenditures. There are large percentage errors in the low income cells but these cells account for a small part of total spending in each category. The expenditure shares in the highest cells also have large percentage errors, but, when the top three cells are aggregated, the errors decline. However, the average percentage errors are larger than in the expenditure ratio case. The details of all cross section comparisons to the 1972 Consumer Expenditure Survey are presented in the next section.

The aggregate demand for each category is the sum of all individual consumer unit demands. The aggregates are calculated by

$$X = \sum X_i = \sum_Y (a + b \cdot \ln YD_i + c \cdot P). \qquad (4.23)$$

As with the total consumption model, the properties of the aggregate demands depend on the income distribution and cannot be studied analytically. Chapter 5 studies the aggregate responses by simulating the models with different macroeconomic assumptions.

Cross Section Model Results

We discuss cross section results for disposable income and expenditures in this separate section because disposable income by income level is the result of two parts of the model, income distribution and taxes. Cross section expenditures are also discussed because they follow directly from disposable income.

Direct comparisons of the cross section disposable income and expenditure detail are not possible over history because the data are not available. However the results for 1972 can be compared with the 1972 Consumer Expenditure Survey (Department of Labor, 1978) in share of aggregate form. (Similar comparison could, in theory, be made using the 1963 Consumer Expenditure Survey.) The percentage of the aggregate variable in each of the twelve income classes for income, disposable income, total expenditures, and the three separate categories of demand predicted by the

Table 4.9. Actual vs. Predicted Aggregate Real Consumer Expenditures

Durables

Date	Actual	Predicted	Difference	% Difference
1960	51.415	54.850	−3.435	−6.681
1961	49.315	57.036	−7.721	−15.657
1962	54.683	59.453	−4.770	−8.724
1963	59.673	62.804	−3.131	−5.246
1964	64.812	67.337	−2.525	−3.895
1965	72.597	72.075	0.522	0.719
1966	78.394	77.042	1.352	1.725
1967	79.476	81.302	−1.826	−2.298
1968	88.335	85.943	2.392	2.708
1969	91.835	89.664	2.171	2.364
1970	89.072	94.623	−5.551	−6.232
1971	98.196	99.207	−1.011	−1.029
1972	111.108	104.779	6.329	5.696
1973	121.323	112.624	8.699	7.170
1974	112.348	116.244	−3.896	−3.468
1975	112.669	120.818	−8.149	−7.233
1976	126.551	125.688	0.863	0.682
1977	137.989	130.840	7.149	5.181
1978	146.808	137.533	9.275	6.318
1979	147.208	142.252	4.956	3.367
1980	137.088	146.568	−9.480	−6.915
1981	140.047	151.570	−11.523	−8.228

Table 4.9. (Continued) Actual vs. Predicted Aggregate Real Consumer Expenditures

Nondurables

Date	Actual	Predicted	Difference	% Difference
1960	208.227	207.792	0.435	0.209
1961	211.937	212.770	−0.833	−0.393
1962	218.500	217.950	0.550	0.252
1963	223.040	226.351	−3.311	−1.484
1964	233.316	235.534	−2.218	−0.951
1965	243.994	244.503	−0.509	−0.209
1966	255.496	250.915	4.581	1.793
1967	259.504	257.251	2.253	0.868
1968	270.500	266.581	3.919	1.449
1969	277.280	272.896	4.384	1.581
1970	283.742	281.398	2.344	0.826
1971	288.672	290.894	−2.222	−0.770
1972	300.638	302.805	−2.167	−0.721
1973	307.967	311.289	−3.322	−1.079
1974	303.298	306.662	−3.364	−1.109
1975	308.226	307.737	0.489	0.159
1976	321.897	318.873	3.024	0.939
1977	333.386	332.980	0.406	0.122
1978	344.395	349.192	−4.798	−1.393
1979	353.071	352.937	0.134	0.038
1980	355.793	355.419	0.374	0.105
1981	362.361	362.616	−0.255	−0.071

Table 4.9. (Continued)   Actual vs. Predicted Aggregate Real Consumer Expenditures

Services

Date	Actual	Predicted	Difference	% Difference
1960	192.399	195.674	-3.275	-1.702
1961	200.155	201.401	-1.246	-0.623
1962	208.828	207.019	1.809	0.866
1963	217.789	217.306	0.483	0.222
1964	229.849	229.331	0.518	0.226
1965	240.890	241.673	-0.783	-0.325
1966	251.793	253.190	-1.397	-0.555
1967	263.675	263.378	0.296	0.112
1968	275.586	276.602	-1.016	-0.369
1969	288.782	286.518	2.264	0.784
1970	299.275	298.862	0.413	0.138
1971	309.921	308.968	0.953	0.308
1972	325.308	321.503	3.805	1.170
1973	339.162	339.278	-0.116	-0.034
1974	347.953	351.685	-3.732	-1.073
1975	359.325	365.724	-6.400	-1.781
1976	374.679	380.537	-5.858	-1.563
1977	392.979	392.721	0.258	0.066
1978	411.999	409.535	2.464	0.598
1979	427.320	421.507	5.813	1.360
1980	437.607	434.253	3.354	0.766
1981	445.248	446.386	-1.138	-0.256

model can be compared with the results of the survey. The comparison must be made in share-of-aggregate form because the survey is a sample, which means that the reported totals are not on the same scale as the reported aggregates. Therefore, to compare model results with the 1972 survey, something must be normalized. This study normalizes both the model results and the 1972 survey into share of aggregate form so that the sum of income class shares for any variable is 100 percent.

The distribution of income for families and unrelated individuals combined is included in this discussion even though the results of the two estimated distributions—families and also unrelated individuals—have already been presented. The combined distribution is discussed here because it is the basis for disposable income and expenditures by income level.

The actual and predicted share of aggregates for the twelve income classes for income, disposable income, and expenditures under both approaches are shown in tables 4.10–4.15.

Income Distributions

The percentage of consumer units in each income class predicted by the model includes both families and unrelated individuals. These results can be compared with the percentage of families by income level in the 1972 Consumer Expenditure Survey because the definition of families used in the survey corresponds closely with the sum of families and unrelated individuals in the model. The predicted values are close to the actual values in the middle-income classes, with larger relative errors in the lower- and upper-income classes. The model underpredicts the percentage of low-income consumer units and overpredicts the percentage of those with high incomes.

The comparison of the distributions of income—income earned in income class—follows this same general pattern. The middle income cells fit somewhat better in percentage error terms than the high and low cells. In terms of aggregate tax and expenditure results, errors in the low income cells will have little impact because small percentages of total income, and therefore taxes and expenditures, come from these income levels. Therefore the 33 percent error in the under $3,000 interval does not represent a large problem.

The 23 percent error in the highest income cell is a potential problem in that this cell has the largest percentage of total income. An error in here could have an impact on aggregate results. However, added together, the four highest income classes include 70 percent of all income and the percentage error for this larger group is only 1.5 percent. In the same way, the four middle-income cells include 21 percent of total income and the percentage error for this group is 1.0 percent. The lowest four income cells include the

Table 4.10. Combined Income Distribution Shares
for Families and Unrelated Individuals

	Income Intervals Constant 1972 Dollars	Percent of Total Income		
		Actual	Predicted	% Error
YPS.CEX1	UNDER $3,000	1.92	2.55	32.30
YPS.CEX2	3,000 TO 4,000	1.73	1.82	5.32
YPS.CEX3	4,000 TO 5,000	2.02	2.27	12.22
YPS.CEX4	5,000 TO 6,000	2.38	2.67	12.31
YPS.CEX5	6,000 TO 7,000	2.73	3.02	10.62
YPS.CEX6	7,000 TO 8,000	3.02	3.32	9.91
YPS.CEX7	8,000 TO 10,000	7.33	7.28	-0.71
YPS.CEX8	10,000 TO 12,000	8.52	7.77	-8.80
YPS.CEX9	12,000 TO 15,000	13.92	11.75	-15.61
YPS.CEX10	15,000 TO 20,000	21.36	17.70	-17.11
YPS.CEX11	20,000 TO 25,000	13.78	13.76	-0.18
YPS.CEX12	OVER 25,000	21.29	26.10	22.61

Table 4.11. Combined Distribution of Disposable Income Shares
for Families and Unrelated Individuals

	Income Intervals Constant 1972 Dollars	Percent of Aggregate Income		
		Actual	Predicted	% Error
YPDS.CEX1	UNDER $3,000	2.16	2.91	34.56
YPDS.CEX2	3,000 TO 4,000	1.95	2.02	3.68
YPDS.CEX3	4,000 TO 5,000	2.24	2.47	10.47
YPDS.CEX4	5,000 TO 6,000	2.43	2.86	17.74
YPDS.CEX5	6,000 TO 7,000	2.94	3.19	8.43
YPDS.CEX6	7,000 TO 8,000	3.18	3.45	8.55
YPDS.CEX7	8,000 TO 10,000	7.59	7.47	-1.55
YPDS.CEX8	10,000 TO 12,000	8.68	7.92	-8.74
YPDS.CEX9	12,000 TO 15,000	14.00	11.90	-15.01
YPDS.CEX10	15,000 TO 20,000	21.16	17.65	-16.59
YPDS.CEX11	20,000 TO 25,000	13.45	13.47	0.16
YPDS.CEX12	OVER 25,000	20.22	24.68	22.06

Table 4.12. Consumption Shares by Income Level— Total Expenditures as Percentage of Aggregate

	Income Intervals Constant 1972 Dollars	Actual	Predicted	% Error
CER.CEX1	UNDER $3,000	5.25	4.25	-18.98
CER.CEX2	3,000 TO 4,000	3.00	2.72	-9.54
CER.CEX3	4,000 TO 5,000	3.12	3.23	3.74
CER.CEX4	5,000 TO 6,000	3.19	3.67	14.79
CER.CEX5	6,000 TO 7,000	3.69	4.02	8.93
CER.CEX6	7,000 TO 8,000	3.80	4.23	11.37
CER.CEX7	8,000 TO 10,000	8.68	8.69	0.14
CER.CEX8	10,000 TO 12,000	9.34	8.67	-7.23
CER.CEX9	12,000 TO 15,000	14.13	12.17	-13.84
CER.CEX10	15,000 TO 20,000	19.88	16.69	-16.07
CER.CEX11	20,000 TO 25,000	11.80	11.76	-0.29
CER.CEX12	OVER 25,000	14.12	19.90	40.93

Table 4.13. Consumption Shares by Income Level— Durable Expenditures as Percentage of Aggregate

	Income Intervals Constant 1972 Dollars	Actual	Predicted	% Error
CEDR.CEX1	UNDER $3,000	3.46	2.61	-24.54
CEDR.CEX2	3,000 TO 4,000	1.92	2.63	36.72
CEDR.CEX3	4,000 TO 5,000	2.29	3.31	44.53
CEDR.CEX4	5,000 TO 6,000	2.35	3.83	62.56
CEDR.CEX5	6,000 TO 7,000	3.28	4.21	28.30
CEDR.CEX6	7,000 TO 8,000	3.45	4.46	29.22
CEDR.CEX7	8,000 TO 10,000	8.15	9.31	14.16
CEDR.CEX8	10,000 TO 12,000	9.75	9.32	-4.36
CEDR.CEX9	12,000 TO 15,000	15.06	13.05	-13.39
CEDR.CEX10	15,000 TO 20,000	21.92	17.50	-20.17
CEDR.CEX11	20,000 TO 25,000	13.37	11.93	-10.77
CEDR.CEX12	OVER 25,000	14.98	17.84	19.12

Table 4.14. Consumption Shares by Income Level — Nondurable Expenditures as Percentage of Aggregate

	Income Intervals Constant 1972 Dollars	Actual	Predicted	% Error
CENR.CEX1	UNDER $3,000	5.16	5.89	13.98
CENR.CEX2	3,000 TO 4,000	3.07	3.63	18.01
CENR.CEX3	4,000 TO 5,000	3.22	4.12	27.81
CENR.CEX4	5,000 TO 6,000	3.34	4.46	33.22
CENR.CEX5	6,000 TO 7,000	3.69	4.67	26.55
CENR.CEX6	7,000 TO 8,000	3.94	4.77	21.26
CENR.CEX7	8,000 TO 10,000	8.88	9.54	7.40
CENR.CEX8	10,000 TO 12,000	9.53	9.15	−3.99
CENR.CEX9	12,000 TO 15,000	14.46	12.33	−14.75
CENR.CEX10	15,000 TO 20,000	20.00	15.90	−20.49
CENR.CEX11	20,000 TO 25,000	11.66	10.49	−10.02
CENR.CEX12	OVER 25,000	13.04	15.06	15.52

Table 4.15. Consumption Shares by Income Level — Services Expenditures as Percentage of Aggregate

	Income Intervals Constant 1972 Dollars	Actual	Predicted	% Error
CESR.CEX1	UNDER $3,000	5.96	5.21	−12.58
CESR.CEX2	3,000 TO 4,000	3.34	3.43	2.64
CESR.CEX3	4,000 TO 5,000	3.33	3.96	18.92
CESR.CEX4	5,000 TO 6,000	3.37	4.33	28.51
CESR.CEX5	6,000 TO 7,000	3.84	4.58	19.04
CESR.CEX6	7,000 TO 8,000	3.81	4.71	23.52
CESR.CEX7	8,000 TO 10,000	8.69	9.49	9.22
CESR.CEX8	10,000 TO 12,000	9.04	9.19	1.63
CESR.CEX9	12,000 TO 15,000	13.51	12.48	−7.63
CESR.CEX10	15,000 TO 20,000	19.04	16.22	−14.78
CESR.CEX11	20,000 TO 25,000	11.34	10.78	−4.92
CESR.CEX12	OVER 25,000	14.73	15.62	6.08

remainder of total income, 9 percent, and the percentage error in this range is 15.7 percent.

The pattern of errors found in comparing the distributions of disposable income is very similar. This is true especially in percent-error terms because disposable income at each income level is roughly a constant multiple (the tax rate) of before tax income.

Comparing disposable income shares predicted by the model to the 1972 Consumer Expenditure Survey shows errors under 9 percent in the middle-income cells and larger errors in the extreme intervals. Again aggregating into three broad ranges reduces errors considerably. The four upper income intervals together account for 69 percent of total disposable income, and the error is 1.6 percent. Similar calculations show that the middle income range covers 22 percent of the total. The prediction error is again 1.6 percent. The lower four classes contain the remainder, 9 percent, and the model overpredicts by 14 percent.

Expenditures

The cross section expenditure results are in general similar to the cross section income distribution results in that the largest relative error occurs in the highest income interval and the smallest percentage errors are found in the middle incomes. Also, when the results are aggregated into three groups, the percentage errors are reduced.

Comparing the two methods of computing consumption — the expenditure ratio approach and the demand equation approach — indicates that the average percent errors (in absolute value terms) are smaller for the expenditure ratio approach. This is expected because the expenditure shares represent twelve parameters — one for each income cell — while in the demand equation method there are only two parameters for each of the three aggregate demand categories.

Expenditure ratio approach. At this point there are two alternative sets of expenditure ratios under consideration. The first set is derived directly from the 1972 Consumer Expenditure data and is shown in table 4.5. The problem is that in the lower income cells, expenditures exceed disposable income. This is questionable because it implies that the consumer's budget constraint is violated. Therefore an alternative set of expenditure ratios is developed and compared. In this case, the budget constraint is assumed to be met and the expenditure ratios are set to under 1.0. The value 0.986 is assumed because it is the first actual expenditure ratio which is under 1.0.

The aggregate results for the two alternatives are very close and differ by no more than 1.4 percent in any year. This is not surprising because the differences in expenditure ratios come in the low-income intervals where there is relatively little income. As a result, the estimated time series relative price equations have differences only in the intercept terms. Choosing between the two alternatives is difficult because the results are similar.

This study will use the expenditure ratios which force the individual budget constraints to hold. Using the constrained alternative will have little impact on middle- and upper-income interval as well as aggregate results because of the small percentage of total expenditures affected. However it will make the low income results easier to interpret and possibly more realistic. For example, if the expenditure ratios exceed 1.0 because of under-reporting of income, tax scenario results could be overstated because taxes presumably apply only to reported income. A tax rate change would have no effect on consumption from unreported income. In addition, with a very high expenditure ratio, a change in consumption could exceed the change in disposable income due to a tax rate change.

Demand equation approach. The cross section errors in the demand equation approach shown by the share of aggregate comparisons for 1972 are larger than in the expenditure ratio method. In the three categories of expenditure, the average percentage error over the twelve income classes is 26 percent for durables, 18 percent for nondurables, and 13 percent for services. Only services compares favorably with the 12 percent average error in the expenditure ratio method.

The likely problem is that the demand equation approach uses semilog Engel curves to capture the distributional effects. These semilog equations have two parameters while each of the 12 expenditure-to-disposable-income ratios can be considered a parameter. More parameters allow a better fit.

However, the three demand equation results are better in percentage error terms than the expenditure ratio results for the upper-income intervals. The reason for this is that all three of the semilog Engel curves under-predict expenditures in the highest two intervals. These errors tend to offset the overprediction of disposable income in these two intervals. Therefore, the two approaches are likely to give different simulation results in the aggregate.

Summary and Conclusion

This chapter presented estimation results for two models of consumer expenditures. Both models rely on the distribution of disposable consumer unit income. To match a reasonable definition of consumer units, it was necessary to fit the distributions of two groups, families and unrelated individuals. Together they form a complete counting of consumer units.

Federal taxes by income level were computed using effective tax rates. These rates were based on yearly IRS tax and income data for tax returns by income level. Tax rates combined with the income distribution yield the distribution of taxes and, therefore, disposable income. In addition, aggregate taxes were computed and compare well with actual collections.

Consumption equations were estimated in two parts. First, consumption income functions were estimated using the cross section 1972 Consumer Expenditure Survey. These equations were then simulated over the distribution of disposable income for the sample period, 1960–1981. This gave time series variables for each expenditure category which were interpreted as the income component of consumption. The differences between the income components and observed values were assumed to be the price components of the expenditure categories.

The second step in estimating the consumption equations explained the price components as functions of relative prices and, in some cases, a time trend variable.

The results of the cross section and time series steps were combined to give expenditure functions for the individual consumer units. The resulting equations have the property of declining marginal propensities to consume in all expenditure categories, as is observed in cross section samples. The time trend terms indicate that individual expenditures rise over time, which implies that the minimum level of consumption is rising over time. Because of the functional forms, price changes affect all consumer units by the same level amount. This drawback is outweighed by the fact that individual consumer units are aggregated consistently.

Aggregate expenditures are computed by evaluating the cross section unit equations over the distribution of disposable income. The aggregates have the advantage of consistent aggregation and do not rely on the much used assumption of the representative consumer with average income. Although theoretically possible, the assumption of identical preferences has not been relaxed.

The final aggregates fit the data well. For the expenditure ratio model, the root mean square error for the sample 1960–1981 is 1.7 percent. For the same period, the root mean square errors for nondurables and services are less than one percent. For durables, this measure of fit is 5 percent.

The two models of aggregate demand estimated in this chapter are a significant advance because aggregation from individual consumer relationships based on micro theory to macroeconomic consumer models is consistent. This is important on a theoretical level because it is a relaxation of the restrictive representative consumer assumption which has been made in many previous studies. On a practical level, the models constructed here may not suffer from a misspecification bias due to the usual assumption of an average consumer with average income. In addition, the models can be used to investigate policies which lead to a change in the distribution of disposable income.

This advance is not without costs. First, the assumption of identical preferences for all consumers is still implicit. Second, the functional forms necessary for consistent aggregation and the two-step procedure for pooling cross section and time series data result in somewhat unrealistic price responses. However this is a small cost in that income determines the major part of expenditures.

5

Historical Simulation and Model Testing

Introduction

This chapter presents simulation results of the consumer spending model which was developed and estimated in the previous chapters. First, the general structure of the model and the simulation methods are described. The purpose is to show how the different parts of the model, the income distribution, tax structure, and consumption equations, fit together. An historical simulation is presented to show how the model predicts over history. Finally, six multiplier experiments are described. The multiplier simulations are used to understand the economic properties of the model.

Presentation of the historical simulation is somewhat repetitive because most of the historical forecast is identical to the predicted values from the estimation results. The reason is that the model structure has almost no feedback of predicted variables.

The estimation results in the previous chapter show that the aggregate variables fit the data well. Expenditures by income level, in share-of-aggregate form were also compared with similar data from the 1972 Consumer Expenditure Survey. These shares of aggregate expenditures are also close to the data but have larger relative errors than the aggregates.

The multiplier analysis serves two purposes. First, the model is simulated with alternative estimated parameters to test the sensitivity of the results to estimation error. The estimated parameters of the income distribution are the foci of these experiments. Second, the results of simulations with exogenous changes in aggregate income can be used to compute aggregate expenditure-income elasticities and marginal propensities to consume in the model. These properties can then be compared with results found in previous studies.

The income and tax rate multiplier simulations will show that the observed properties of the expenditure ratio method are acceptable when compared to previous studies. However, the calculated aggregate marginal propensities to consume in the demand equation approach are shown to be out of the acceptable range. Therefore results from the demand equation method are not considered in later simulations.

Simulation of the Model

Simulation of the model uses a straightforward top-down computation method. Aggregate income, prices, tax rates, and parameters of the income distribution are taken exogenously. The model computes taxes, disposable income, and consumer expenditures for consumer units at different levels of income over the full income range. Cross section results are then summed using the income distribution to determine weights—the number of consumer units at each income level. Summing gives taxes and expenditures in twelve income intervals as well as aggregate totals.

More specifically, the model evaluates taxes and expenditures at 239 income levels ranging from $75 to approximately ten times aggregate mean income. (Income intervals are measured in constant 1972 dollars.) The upper limit is chosen because, when the gamma income distribution function is evaluated at ten times mean income, its value is zero. Evaluating the tax and expenditure equations at higher incomes would have no effect. The implication is that there are no consumers with income greater than ten times the aggregate mean income. The only published income distribution data detailed enough to test this are tax return data. For example, in 1972, the latest year in which an appropriate income interval is reported, average adjusted gross income was $9,600. In that year 99.3% of all tax returns reported incomes under $100,000, approximately ten times the average.

The income levels can be interpreted as the income of a representative consumer in each of 239 income cells. The size of the intervals is small, $150, in the low income levels where there is the greatest concentration of consumer units and it is larger, up to $3,750, at high income levels where there are fewer consumers. Variable income intervals are used to reduce the number of computations.

For each of the 239 income cells, taxes, disposable income, and expenditures for the representative consumer are computed. Then, the income distribution is evaluated and the result is used to approximate the number of consumers in each income cell. Multiplying taxes and expenditures for the representative consumer by the number of consumer units gives the totals for these variables in the income cell. This process is repeated for all of the income cells and the results are summed to twelve income intervals, which give the model's cross section detail, and these are summed to give the aggregate results.

Model Structure

The details of the model structure closely follow the estimation procedure described in the previous chapter. However, there are some details such as accounting identities which need to be made clear. The following sections outline the equations used to determine the tax and expenditure variables on a consumer unit basis. The discussion begins with the aggregate income inputs and ends with the determination of the aggregate results.

Aggregate Income

The key income variable used is based on the adjusted gross income concept, which can be derived from national income accounts data. It is defined as

$$AGI\$ = YP\$ - TRTOP\$ + TXCSTP\$ \qquad (5.1)$$

where $YP\$$ is personal income, $TRTOP\$$ are transfer payments, and $TXCSTP\$$ are personal contributions to social insurance. The reason for using adjusted gross income is that it is the basis for personal federal taxes. In addition, disposable income, which is necessary in determining consumption, can easily be calculated using adjusted gross income. For the exact derivation of adjusted gross income from personal income, see Pechman (1977).

The use of adjusted gross income is a potential problem because the estimated parameters of the distributions of income are based on family income. Family income includes transfer payments which are excluded from adjusted gross income. However, because of the way in which transfers are handled (discussed below), this is a small problem. Other differences and problems in the income definitions are discussed in "Money Income of Households, Families, and Persons in the United States: 1980," U.S. Department of Commerce, Bureau of the Census.

Taxes

Each consumer unit is assumed to pay three types of personal income tax: federal, state and local, and contributions to social insurance. The federal tax rates depend on income level and are based on historical effective tax rates which account for all of the complexities in the law.

The state and local personal tax rates are assumed to be a flat rate for all consumers. For each year of the historical sample the flat tax rate is computed as total state and local revenues divided by income, where income is defined as adjusted gross income. This calculation is an oversimplification because some state income taxes are progressive and are not necessarily based on the adjusted gross income concept. Other states do not have an income tax.

The social security tax is based on the actual law. For income levels below the maximum earnings, the tax is the statutory rate times the income level, and, for income levels above the maximum, the maximum tax is charged. The simplifying assumption used in the model is that all income is subject to the social security tax while only wage earnings are actually subject to the tax.

Disposable Income

Given adjusted gross income and the three taxes mentioned above, disposable income is almost completely determined. The missing variable is transfer payments, the aggregate of which is taken exogenously. In order to include transfers in disposable income, some assumption on the distribution of transfers by income level must be made. This study assumes that transfers are distributed in the same way as all other income because the data from which the income distribution parameters were estimated included transfer payments.

Disposable income at each income level is then expressed as

$$YD\$ = AGI\$ + TRTOP\$ - TXCPF\$ - TXCPS\$ - TXCSTP\$ \quad (5.2)$$

where $TXCPF\$$ are personal federal taxes, $TXCPS\$$ are personal state taxes, and $TXCSTPS\$$ are contributions to social insurance.

Expenditures

After disposable income is known, expenditures for consumer units at each income level are calculated. At this point the two approaches to consumer expenditures differ. The expenditure ratio model calculates expenditures by the equation

$$CE_i = a_1 \cdot \text{time} + b_i \, YD_i + \sum_{t=0}^{-2} c_t \cdot r_t \quad (5.3)$$

where CE_i are expenditures of consumer unit i, time is the time trend, and r_t is the after-tax rate of return, at each of the 239 income levels.

Alternatively, the demand equation model calculates demand for each of the three identified goods by equations of the form

$$X_i = a_0 + a_1 \cdot \text{time} + b \cdot \ln YD_i + c \cdot PX/P \qquad (5.4)$$

where X_i is the demand for good x by consumer unit i and PX/P is the relative price of good x. The estimated equations are shown in chapter 4.

Income Distribution

After these calculations are made, the cross section and aggregate results are computed using the number of consumer units in each income cell from the income distribution. For each income cell, the number of consumer units is the sum of the number of families and unrelated individuals, which are computed by evaluating the density functions for families and unrelated individuals. The number of consumer units is then

$$NT_I \int_{Y_I} f_F (\cdot)dy + f_u(\cdot)dy \qquad (5.5)$$

where NT_I is the number of consumer units in income cell I, f_F is the gamma distribution for families, and f_u is the gamma distribution for unrelated individuals.

After this process has been repeated for all 239 income cells, the aggregates for the tax and expenditure variables are calculated as weighted sums.

Historical Simulation

Presentation of the historical simulation is somewhat repetitive because the predicted aggregate variables which have been directly estimated are the same as the estimation results presented in chapter 4. The reason for the similarity is that there is no feedback in the model. Therefore, this section summarizes the simulation results which have already been discussed, and

Table 5.1.   Summary of Historical
Simulation Errors

Expenditure Ratio Method	
Total Consumption	1.33

Demand Equation Method	
Total Consumption	0.97
Durables	5.08
Nondurables	0.84
Services	0.85

presents those results, such as savings, which are derived from the estimated equations.

Aggregate Results

Table 5.2 gives the aggregate historical results. The three personal taxes are calculated in nominal terms using the income distribution. Disposable income and consumer expenditures using both methods are then shown in constant dollars. Finally, savings under the two alternative approaches to expenditures are shown.

As discussed previously, the key variables follow history closely. For personal federal taxes, the largest error occurs in 1975 when the model over-predicts revenues by $12.6 billion. The most likely cause is that 1975 was a recession year in which real income as measured by the GNP fell and the unemployment rate increased. As a result, income per family and per individual fell, and both distributions of income shifted to the left. The shift results in lower tax collections predicted by the model because of greater weight in the lower income intervals. However, the reduction is not as great as the observed drop and therefore the overprediction is large.

Conversely, 1972 was a boom year with increases in per family and per individual income. This caused the income distributions to shift to the right, increasing predicted collections. However, actual tax collections increased more, and underprediction results.

The fact that taxes for all years except 1972 are overpredicted indicates a bias in the calculation method. The most likely reason is an overprediction of income in the upper-income levels by the income distribution as was discussed in chapter 4. To account for this bias, the tax rates used in the estimation and simulation of the distribution of disposable income and expenditures were adjusted by approximately 5 percent, such that aggregate tax collections were predicted exactly. The impact of this adjustment on estimated coefficients was tested. Only the intercept term or time trend coefficient changed. Therefore federal taxes used in estimation and simulation follow history exactly.

The aggregate expenditure variables, total expenditures, and also the three components, predict history more closely. This is not surprising because all of the expenditure variables are the result of least squares regression rather than the result of a computation process as is the case with personal federal taxes. Recall that expenditures in both the expenditure ratio and demand equation approaches are predicted by regression equations which have as explanatory variables relative price terms and an income variable which is calculated using the income distribution and cross section equations.

For the aggregates, total expenditures predicted by the expenditure ratio approach fit the observed data well with a root mean square percent error of 1.33. The largest single relative errors are overpredictions in 1974 and 1975. Although these are both low aggregate growth years, there is no obvious pattern in the errors as there was in personal taxes.

The demand equation approach also produces good aggregate results. However, there are some large errors in the durables category, which result in a root mean square percent error of 5.08. Services and nondurables fit more closely and have root mean square percent errors under 0.9.

The errors for total expenditures under the demand equation approach are also small with a root mean square percent error of 0.97, which is less than the same measure under the expenditure ratio approach. The largest single year relative errors occur in 1961, 1974 and 1975. In each of these years, actual real expenditures grew more slowly than the historical average and actually fell in 1974. There are also overpredictions in 1980 and 1981, which were slow growth years. These errors indicate that the demand equation approach might overpredict total expenditures in slack periods.

Aggregate Savings

Savings do not fit the data as well in percentage error terms. The savings residuals are identical (except of opposite sign) to the expenditure residuals because savings is the difference between disposable income and spending. Predicted disposable income does not equal the actual even though taxes are predicted perfectly, because income by income level does not sum to aggregate income exactly due to an approximation error in the integration. The error in income is small, less than 0.4 percent, but because savings is small relative to income, the error in savings becomes significant. Therefore these savings calculations use actual disposable income. In comparing simulations later on, predicted disposable income will be used in both cases and the bias will cancel out. Therefore, because the level of savings is small compared to consumption, the percentage errors in savings are large.

In addition, the patterns of the savings residuals are the same as in expenditures. Therefore, that both models overpredict spending in low growth years indicates that both underpredict savings in these years.

Cross Section Results

The historical simulation also includes cross section detail for income, disposable income, and consumer expenditures. These results, however, are somewhat difficult to compare with history because of data problems. The cross section before-tax income distribution data are available for families and unrelated individuals over the historical sample and are compared with the predicted distributions in the estimation section of chapter 4. In that chapter, it was reported that the estimated distributions fit the observed distributions well in the middle-income range, but there are some large errors in the upper-income levels in some years.

Direct comparisons of the cross section disposable income and expenditures historical simulation results are not possible because the data are not available. For these variables, however, the share of aggregates in the twelve income intervals can be compared with the 1972 Consumer Expenditure Survey. The comparisons were shown in chapter 4. To summarize the results, the shares of disposable income in the twelve income intervals were close to the 1972 survey in most cases. The middle intervals had the smallest percentage errors, most of which were under 10 percent. Larger errors occurred in the lowest and highest intervals. However, when aggregated into three income ranges, the middle and upper ranges had small percentage errors and the lowest income range had a much larger relative error. The lower-income intervals affect aggregate results only slightly because only a small percentage of income falls in the low income range. The expenditure share of aggregate results follow the same pattern.

Aggregate Factors Affecting Cross Section Results

Tables 5.2 and 5.3 show the aggregate variables in the model. Table 5.2 shows adjusted gross income, the population statistics, prices, and the income distribution parameter alpha, which are exogenous inputs in the model. Income is divided among families and unrelated individuals using a share ratio derived from the data. The model then computes mean incomes for the two groups and then converts them into 1972 dollars using the consumer price deflator.

Reviewing table 5.2 shows that personal income and adjusted gross income increased in nominal terms over the period 1960 through 1981. However, in constant dollars, both income measures fell in 1974. Adjusted gross income fell again in 1975 and 1980.

The population statistics, the number of families and the number of unrelated individuals, increased over the sample. However, not only did both populations increase, but the ratio of persons living alone to families increased. Together with the drops in real income, these trends have a significant impact on the result and can be seen through the impacts on average real income.

Declines in aggregate real income and the changes in demographics hold down average real income. In 1973, average real income for all consumer units was $13,100 and in 1974 it fell to $12,500 because both aggregate real income fell and the number of consumer units increased. By 1976, aggregate real income was above the 1973 level, but growth in the number of consumers held average real income to $12,300. The average did not reach the 1973 level until 1979 even though aggregate real income was rising. The same pattern occurred in 1980 when the average fell to $12,700 because of a drop in aggregate real income and an increase in the number of consumer units.

In addition to increases in the total number of consumer units, the mix has been shifting toward unrelated individuals. In 1960, the ratio of persons living alone to families was 0.25 and by 1981 this ratio grew to 0.45. The trend is important because it means that there is a greater percentage of lower-income consumer units than there would have been had this shift not occurred.

Three factors — changes in real aggregate income, increases in the total number of consumer units, and a shift toward persons living alone who have lower average incomes — affected the distribution of income in the base simulation. The effects can be seen in the predicted combined income distribution results shown in tables 5.4 and 5.5. The general trend over the period 1960–1981 has been a shift toward the higher income classes. However, this trend was broken in 1970, 1974 and 1979 due to the factors discussed above which reduced real average income. For example, in 1960 the model predicted that 3.9 percent of income was earned in the under $3,000 range. By 1969, this figure had fallen to 2.3 percent. However, in 1970 the trend in the distribution of real income was reversed and 2.5 percent of income fell in the under $3,000 class. Similar declines, then upward shifts, occurred in 1974 and again in 1979. At the other end of the scale, the percentage of income in the highest income class increased from 12.5 percent in 1960 to 28.5 percent in 1981 with several dips over the period.

The shift in the composition of consumer units toward a greater percentage of unrelated individuals has reduced average income because unrelated individuals have a lower average income. This movement has lowered the combined average income and shifted the income distribution toward lower incomes. However, that the income distribution shows a larger percentage of income in the lower-income levels does not necessarily indicate a poorer society. Rather, the increase in the relative number of persons living alone could indicate a better-off society which allows persons to live alone rather than with a family. The effects of this are examined below in a simulation which fixes the ratio of families to unrelated individuals at the 1960 level.

Table 5.2. Aggregate Historical Inputs

	1960	1961	1962	1963	1964	1965	1966	1967	1968	1969	1970	1971
INCOME MEASURES												
YP$ PERSONAL INCOME	402.3	417.8	443.6	466.2	499.2	540.7	588.2	630.0	690.6	754.7	811.1	868.4
AGI$ ADJUSTED GROSS INCOME	382.7	394.7	420.2	442.1	474.3	513.6	561.3	598.0	653.6	714.3	758.8	804.7
AGI ADJUSTED GROSS INCOME CONSTANT 1972 DOLLARS	532.4	543.6	570.1	590.8	625.4	665.3	706.8	735.2	772.4	807.7	820.3	834.1
POPULATION STATISTICS												
NTOT "CONSUMER UNITS"	56.2	56.8	58.0	58.4	59.0	60.3	61.1	61.9	63.5	65.0	66.6	67.7
NCF FAMILIES	45.1	45.5	46.4	47.1	47.5	48.0	48.5	49.2	50.1	50.8	51.6	52.1
NCU UNRELATED	11.1	11.2	11.6	11.3	11.4	12.3	12.6	12.7	13.4	14.2	15.0	15.6
MEANT HOUSEHOLD MEAN INCOME	9.5	9.6	9.8	10.1	10.6	11.0	11.6	11.9	12.2	12.4	12.3	12.3
FAMILY INCOME DISTRIBUTION												
MEANF MEAN INCOME	10.7	10.8	11.5	11.5	11.9	12.5	13.2	13.5	13.9	14.3	14.2	14.3
ALPHAF ALPHA PARAMETER	2.19	2.11	2.22	2.22	2.25	2.29	2.44	2.40	2.46	2.44	2.36	2.37
BETAF BETA PARAMETER	4.9	5.1	5.2	5.2	5.3	5.5	5.4	5.6	5.6	5.9	6.0	6.0
UNRELATED INDIVIDUAL INCOME DISTRIBUTION												
MEANU MEAN INCOME	4.3	4.4	3.0	4.6	5.0	5.2	5.3	5.4	5.7	5.7	5.8	5.9
ALPHAU ALPHA PARAMETER	1.00	1.00	1.00	1.00	1.00	1.00	1.04	1.02	1.17	1.19	1.26	1.33
BETAU BETA PARAMETER	4.3	4.4	3.0	4.6	5.0	5.2	5.1	5.3	4.9	4.8	4.6	4.4
PRICES, RELATIVE TO ALL CONSUMER GOODS												
RPDCED DURABLES	1.17	1.16	1.16	1.15	1.15	1.12	1.09	1.08	1.08	1.06	1.03	1.03
RPDCEN NONDURABLES	1.01	1.01	1.00	1.00	1.00	1.00	1.01	1.01	1.01	1.01	1.01	1.00
RPDCES SERVICES	.94	.95	.96	.96	.96	.96	.96	.97	.97	.97	.98	.99
INTEREST RATE												
LONGRR AFTER TAX REAL	2.33	3.12	2.58	2.42	2.76	2.38	1.89	2.73	1.68	1.89	2.86	2.76

	1972	1973	1974	1975	1976	1977	1978	1979	1980	1981
INCOME MEASURES										
YP$ PERSONAL INCOME	951.4	1065.2	1168.6	1265.0	1391.2	1540.4	1732.7	1951.2	2160.4	2415.8
AGI$ ADJUSTED GROSS INCOME	881.1	988.3	1075.3	1137.1	1252.4	1393.6	1578.6	1782.0	1951.9	2184.4
AGI ADJUSTED GROSS INCOME CONSTANT 1972 DOLLARS	881.2	935.4	924.5	908.5	950.7	1000.1	1058.9	1096.8	1089.4	1123.1
POPULATION STATISTICS										
"CONSUMER UNITS"										
NTOT FAMILIES	69.7	71.3	73.9	75.2	77.4	79.1	82.1	83.7	86.0	87.7
NCF UNRELATED	53.2	54.5	55.2	56.1	56.8	57.6	58.3	59.3	59.6	60.3
NCU	16.5	16.8	18.7	19.2	20.5	21.6	23.8	24.4	26.4	27.3
MEANT HOUSEHOLD MEAN INCOME	12.6	13.1	12.5	12.1	12.3	12.6	12.9	13.1	12.7	12.8
FAMILY INCOME DISTRIBUTION										
MEANF MEAN INCOME	14.7	15.2	14.6	14.1	14.5	14.9	15.4	15.7	15.2	15.5
ALPHAF ALPHA PARAMETER	2.34	2.39	2.29	2.33	2.33	2.26	2.26	2.16	2.14	2.14
BETAF BETA PARAMETER	6.3	6.4	6.4	6.1	6.2	6.6	6.8	7.3	7.1	7.2
UNRELATED INDIVIDUAL INCOME DISTRIBUTION										
MEANU MEAN INCOME	6.0	6.4	6.2	6.0	6.2	6.5	6.8	6.9	6.9	6.9
ALPHAU ALPHA PARAMETER	1.37	1.44	1.60	1.55	1.56	1.65	1.62	1.64	1.64	1.60
BETAU BETA PARAMETER	4.4	4.4	3.9	3.9	4.0	4.0	4.2	4.2	4.2	4.3
PRICES, RELATIVE TO ALL CONSUMER GOODS										
RPDCED DURABLES	1.00	.96	.93	.94	.94	.93	.91	.89	.87	.86
RPDCEN NONDURABLES	1.00	1.03	1.06	1.06	1.04	1.03	1.03	1.05	1.05	1.04
RPDCES SERVICES	1.00	.99	.97	.97	.98	1.00	1.01	1.00	1.00	1.01
INTEREST RATE										
LONGRR AFTER TAX REAL	3.04	1.23	-2.16	.90	2.69	1.62	.96	-.26	.79	4.45

Table 5.3.　Selected Aggregate Indicators

		1960	1961	1962	1963	1964	1965	1966	1967	1968	1969	1970	1971
	PERSONAL TAXES												
TXCPF$	FEDERAL	43.6	44.7	48.6	51.5	48.6	53.9	61.7	67.5	79.7	95.1	92.6	90.3
TXCPS$	STATE AND LOCAL	6.7	7.4	8.2	8.9	10.0	11.0	12.9	14.7	17.6	20.7	23.3	26.5
TXCSTP$	SOCIAL SECURITY PERSONAL CONTRIBUTION	6.5	6.5	6.9	8.3	8.6	8.8	13.5	14.5	17.3	19.5	20.1	22.5
	INCOME MEASURES CONSTANT DOLLARS												
YP	PERSONAL INCOME	559.7	575.5	602.0	622.9	658.1	700.3	740.7	774.5	816.0	853.4	876.8	900.2
YPD	DISPOSABLE INCOME	495.6	510.2	531.6	549.4	588.8	625.2	655.7	684.6	711.8	734.2	764.1	791.9
	CONSUMER EXPENDITURES CONSTANT DOLLARS												
	EXPENDITURE RATIO METHOD												
CE	TOTAL EXPENDITURES	460.8	470.9	485.7	502.5	532.2	560.5	584.1	605.9	630.4	648.5	674.9	699.0
	DEMAND EQUATION METHOD												
CED	DURABLES	54.9	57.0	59.5	62.8	67.3	72.1	77.0	81.3	85.9	89.7	94.6	99.2
CEN	NON-DURABLES	207.8	212.8	217.9	226.4	235.5.	244.5	250.9	257.3	266.6	272.9	281.4	290.9
CES	SERVICES	195.7	201.4	207.0	217.3	229.3	241.7	253.4	263.4	276.6	286.5	298.9	309.0
CET	TOTAL	458.3	471.2	484.4	506.5	532.2	558.3	581.1	601.9	629.1	649.1	674.9	699.1
	CURRENT DOLLARS SAVINGS												
SAVE1$	EXPENDITURE RATIO METHOD	25.0	28.5	33.9	35.1	43.0	49.9	56.9	64.0	68.9	75.8	82.5	89.6
SAVE2$	DEMAND EQUATION METHOD	26.8	28.3	34.8	32.1	43.0	51.7	59.2	67.2	70.0	75.3	82.5	89.5

		1972	1973	1974	1975	1976	1977	1978	1979	1980	1981
	PERSONAL TAXES										
TXCPF$	FEDERAL	108.2	114.7	131.3	125.8	147.3	170.1	194.9	230.6	257.5	298.1
TXCPS$	STATE AND LOCAL	33.0	36.2	39.0	43.3	49.8	56.6	64.1	70.8	79.2	89.1
TXCSTP$	SOCIAL SECURITY	26.1	35.2	42.0	45.5	50.3	55.5	64.4	79.8	89.8	111.1
	PERSONAL CONTRIBUTION INCOME MEASURES CONSTANT DOLLARS										
YP	PERSONAL INCOME	951.4	1008.2	1004.8	1010.7	1056.1	1105.5	1162.3	1200.9	1205.8	1242.1
YPD	DISPOSABLE INCOME	823.1	877.3	868.1	884.3	915.4	952.0	997.5	1021.6	1022.5	1045.2
	CONSUMER EXPENDITURES CONSTANT DOLLARS										
	EXPENDITURE RATIO METHOD										
CE	TOTAL EXPENDITURES	723.1	767.4	779.9	802.3	824.9	851.7	888.4	911.9	923.8	934.8
	DEMAND EQUATION METHOD										
CED	DURABLES	104.8	112.6	116.2	120.8	125.7	130.8	137.5	142.3	146.6	151.6
CEN	NON-DURABLES	302.8	311.3	306.7	307.7	318.9	333.0	349.2	352.9	355.4	362.6
CES	SERVICES	321.5	339.3	351.7	365.7	380.5	392.7	409.5	421.5	434.3	446.4
CET	TOTAL	729.1	763.2	774.6	794.3	825.1	856.5	896.3	916.7	936.2	960.6
	CURENT DOLLAR SAVINGS										
SAVE1$	EXPENDITURE RATIO	100.0	116.1	102.5	102.6	119.2	139.8	162.6	178.1	176.9	214.8
SAVE2$	DEMAND EQUATION METHOD	94.0	120.6	108.8	112.7	118.9	133.0	150.9	170.4	154.6	164.7

Table 5.4. Combined Income Distribution for Families and Unrelated Individuals — Constant 1972 Dollars

		1960	1961	1962	1963	1964	1965	1966	1967	1968	1969	1970	1971
	INCOME INTERVALS CONSTANT 1972 DOLLARS												
YP.CEX1	UNDER $3,000	22.2	23.5	24.6	22.0	20.7	20.5	19.3	20.1	20.0	20.8	23.1	24.4
YP.CEX2	3,000 TO 4,000	16.4	16.9	16.0	16.1	15.4	15.1	14.2	14.4	14.8	15.1	16.6	17.5
YP.CEX3	4,000 TO 5,000	20.5	20.9	19.5	20.3	19.6	19.2	18.3	18.5	19.0	19.2	20.9	22.0
YP.CEX4	5,000 TO 6,000	23.9	24.2	22.6	23.9	23.4	22.9	22.2	22.4	23.0	23.1	24.8	26.0
YP.CEX5	6,000 TO 7,000	26.6	26.7	25.1	26.9	26.5	26.1	25.7	25.8	26.6	26.6	28.3	29.5
YP.CEX6	7,000 TO 8,000	28.5	28.5	27.1	29.1	28.9	28.7	28.6	28.7	29.6	29.7	31.2	32.4
YP.CEX7	8,000 TO 10,000	59.6	59.6	57.8	62.0	62.4	62.7	63.5	63.9	66.1	66.3	68.9	71.2
YP.CEX8	10,000 TO 12,000	59.2	59.2	59.0	62.9	64.4	65.7	67.9	68.6	71.3	71.8	73.7	75.8
YP.CEX9	12,000 TO 15,000	80.7	81.2	83.5	88.3	92.2	95.8	101.1	103.1	107.7	109.3	111.1	113.9
YP.CEX10	15,000 TO 20,000	102.1	104.2	112.1	116.8	125.3	134.1	145.4	150.6	158.9	164.0	165.3	168.9
YP.CEX11	20,000 TO 25,000	62.9	65.8	74.2	76.1	84.4	93.6	104.2	110.6	118.0	124.8	125.6	128.2
YP.CEX12	OVER 25,000	72.1	80.1	96.8	96.7	114.3	136.2	156.2	176.6	192.1	216.7	221.9	226.6
YP	AGGREGATE INCOME	574.7	590.9	618.1	641.2	677.5	720.7	766.6	803.4	847.1	887.3	911.2	936.3

		1972	1973	1974	1975	1976	1977	1978	1979	1980	1981
	INCOME INTERVALS CONSTANT 1972 DOLLARS										
YP.CEX1	UNDER $3,000	25.2	24.2	27.8	31.7	32.2	31.5	31.8	32.9	36.4	37.8
YP.CEX2	3,000 TO 4,000	18.0	17.8	20.7	22.8	23.1	23.3	23.4	24.1	26.3	26.7
YP.CEX3	4,000 TO 5,000	22.4	22.4	25.7	27.9	28.4	28.7	28.9	29.5	32.0	32.4
YP.CEX4	5,000 TO 6,000	26.4	26.6	30.0	32.4	32.9	33.3	33.6	34.1	36.7	37.1
YP.CEX5	6,000 TO 7,000	29.9	30.3	33.6	36.1	36.6	37.0	37.4	37.9	40.5	40.8
YP.CEX6	7,000 TO 8,000	32.8	33.4	36.5	38.9	39.6	40.0	40.5	40.8	43.3	43.7
YP.CEX7	8,000 TO 10,000	72.1	73.9	78.8	83.6	85.2	85.8	87.4	87.5	92.2	93.0
YP.CEX8	10,000 TO 12,000	77.0	79.6	82.7	87.0	88.8	89.5	91.6	91.4	95.2	96.3
YP.CEX9	12,000 TO 15,000	116.4	121.7	123.0	127.8	131.2	132.6	136.6	136.2	140.0	142.1
YP.CEX10	15,000 TO 20,000	175.3	186.1	182.5	185.5	192.3	196.7	204.9	205.6	207.2	212.0
YP.CEX11	20,000 TO 25,000	136.3	147.2	140.7	138.6	145.9	152.7	161.6	164.9	162.6	168.1
YP.CEX12	OVER 25,000	258.5	290.3	268.8	243.4	267.0	303.5	336.7	371.2	348.4	371.3
YP	AGGREGATE INCOME	990.4	1053.5	1050.8	1055.8	1103.2	1154.5	1214.5	1256.1	1260.6	1301.4

Table 5.5. Combined Income Distribution Shares for Families and Unrelated Individuals – Percent of Total Income

	INCOME INTERVALS CONSTANT 1972 DOLLARS	1960	1961	1962	1963	1964	1965	1966	1967	1968	1969	1970	1971
YP.CEX1	UNDER $3,000	3.9	4.0	4.0	3.4	3.1	2.8	2.5	2.5	2.4	2.3	2.5	2.6
YP.CEX2	3,000 TO 4,000	2.9	2.9	2.6	2.5	2.3	2.1	1.9	1.8	1.7	1.7	1.8	1.9
YP.CEX3	4,000 TO 5,000	3.6	3.5	3.1	3.2	2.9	2.7	2.4	2.3	2.2	2.2	2.3	2.3
YP.CEX4	5,000 TO 6,000	4.2	4.1	3.7	3.7	3.4	3.2	2.9	2.8	2.7	2.6	2.7	2.8
YP.CEX5	6,000 TO 7,000	4.6	4.5	4.1	4.2	3.9	3.6	3.3	3.2	3.1	3.0	3.1	3.1
YP.CEX6	7,000 TO 8,000	5.0	4.8	4.4	4.5	4.3	4.0	3.7	3.6	3.5	3.3	3.4	3.5
YP.CEX7	8,000 TO 10,000	10.4	10.1	9.3	9.7	9.2	8.7	8.3	8.0	7.8	7.5	7.6	7.6
YP.CEX8	10,000 TO 12,000	10.3	10.0	9.5	9.8	9.5	9.1	8.9	8.5	8.4	8.1	8.1	8.1
YP.CEX9	12,000 TO 15,000	14.0	13.7	13.5	13.8	13.6	13.3	13.2	12.8	12.7	12.3	12.2	12.2
YP.CEX10	15,000 TO 20,000	17.8	17.6	18.1	18.2	18.5	18.6	19.0	18.8	18.8	18.5	18.1	18.0
YP.CEX11	20,000 TO 25,000	10.9	11.1	12.0	11.9	12.5	13.0	13.6	13.8	13.9	14.1	13.8	13.7
YP.CEX12	OVER 25,000	12.5	13.5	15.7	15.1	16.9	18.9	20.4	22.0	22.7	24.4	24.4	24.2

		1972	1973	1974	1975	1976	1977	1978	1979	1980	1981
	INCOME INTERVALS CONSTANT 1972 DOLLARS										
YP.CEX1	UNDER $3,000	2.5	2.3	2.6	3.0	2.9	2.7	2.6	2.6	2.9	2.9
YP.CEX2	3,000 TO 4,000	1.8	1.7	2.0	2.2	2.1	2.0	1.9	1.9	2.1	2.1
YP.CEX3	4,000 TO 5,000	2.3	2.1	2.4	2.6	2.6	2.5	2.4	2.3	2.5	2.5
YP.CEX4	5,000 TO 6,000	2.7	2.5	2.9	3.1	3.0	2.9	2.8	2.7	2.9	2.8
YP.CEX5	6,000 TO 7,000	3.0	2.9	3.2	3.4	3.3	3.2	3.1	3.0	3.2	3.1
YP.CEX6	7,000 TO 8,000	3.3	3.2	3.5	3.7	3.6	3.5	3.3	3.2	3.4	3.4
YP.CEX7	8,000 TO 10,000	7.3	7.0	7.5	7.9	7.7	7.4	7.2	7.0	7.3	7.1
YP.CEX8	10,000 TO 12,000	7.8	7.6	7.9	8.2	8.1	7.8	7.5	7.3	7.6	7.4
YP.CEX9	12,000 TO 15,000	11.8	11.5	11.7	12.1	11.9	11.5	11.3	10.8	11.1	10.9
YP.CEX10	15,000 TO 20,000	17.7	17.7	17.4	17.6	17.4	17.0	16.9	16.4	16.4	16.3
YP.CEX11	20,000 TO 25,000	13.8	14.0	13.4	13.1	13.2	13.2	13.3	13.1	12.9	12.9
YP.CEX12	OVER 25,000	26.1	27.6	25.6	23.1	24.2	26.3	27.7	29.5	27.6	28.5

Sensitivity Analysis

The simulations can be divided into three groups. First discussed is a multiplier simulation which increases aggregate income for both families and unrelated individuals by 10 percent. The inequality of the distributions are preserved, but both are shifted due to higher average incomes. This run differs from the demographic experiments in that they can be compared with the results of more traditional models.

The second group contains simulations which directly test the sensitivity of the cross section assumptions in the model. Included is a simulation which tests the sensitivity of the model results to change in the breakdown of income and consumer units into families and unrelated individuals. The other demographic simulation tests the sensitivity of results to changes in the estimated income distribution parameters which alter the variance of the income distributions.

Finally, there are three tax rate simulations. In these runs, the model's responses to alternative tax rate structures are analyzed. These simulations provide a basis for the tax policy scenarios in the next chapter. Two tax rate sensitivity runs cut aggregate personal federal taxes by 10 percent, but in different ways. The first is an across the board rate reduction while the second reduces upper-income tax rates such that aggregate taxes fall by 10 percent. These alternatives are compared to study the aggregate and cross section model responses to tax rate shifts. The last tax simulation redistributes taxes from high- to low-income consumers while attempting to keep aggregate taxes at base levels. This run indicates what might be expected from a flat tax scenario, and how the results might come about.

Ten Percent Increase in Income Simulation

The income multiplier simulation shows the direct effects on taxes and expenditures of a 10 percent increase in income. This simulation differs from the demographic simulations because the outcomes can be compared with the results of similar shocks given to more traditional average consumer models.

The income simulation is of specific interest because the results can be used to calculate the total expenditure-income properties of the model. The marginal propensity to consume and the expenditure income elasticity will be discussed. These properties are important because they summarize consumer behavior.

The income response properties cannot be determined analytically in both approaches to consumer expenditures considered here because they depend on cross section equations and the distribution of income. In the expenditure ratio approach, for example, the marginal propensity to consume is 0.986 for the lowest income consumer units, and it declines to 0.56 for the highest income consumers.

The marginal propensities for the three demand equations also decline as the level of income rises. The general form of the demand equations is

$$X_i = a + b \cdot \ln YD_i + C \cdot P. \tag{5.6}$$

This results in a marginal propensity equation

$$dX_i/dYD_i = b/YD_i. \tag{5.7}$$

Thus, the individual consumer unit marginal propensities to consume depend on the income coefficient and the level of disposable income.

The simulation increases the aggregate adjusted gross income input into the model by 10 percent over the historical base. All of the other inputs are kept the same. This causes the major aggregates, taxes and expenditures, to go up.

Results

In the cross section, before-tax income increases in the upper-income classes, roughly those above $10,000 (1972 dollars), but income declines in the lower intervals. All incomes rise, shifting consumer units up in their own brackets or into the next bracket. Higher aggregate income increases the average income for both the family and unrelated individual groups, shifting the income distributions to the right. However, it does not affect the skewness of the distributions. Recall that with a fixed alpha parameter, the skewness of the gamma distribution does not change.

Taxes. The increase in aggregate income and the shift in the distribution together cause federal personal taxes to rise. Over the period 1960 to 1981, personal taxes increase by 15.6 percent on average compared with the base case. It is interesting to note that the percentage increase is very stable over the sample and is an additional indication that the progressive nature of tax rates has not changed very much over the years.

It is also interesting to note that a 10 percent increase in income results in a greater than 10 percent increase in taxes. This shows that the tax structure is progressive. A simple linear tax equation would yield a percentage change in taxes identical to the income change.

The 15.6 percent tax increase is validated by Pechman (1977, p. 12). He observed that "under the rates in effect in 1977, federal individual tax receipts automatically increase or decrease by about 15 percent for every 10 percent increase or decrease in personal income."

As a result of the increase in income, aggregate disposable income increases over the base case by an average of 8.3 percent. The percentage increase declines over the sample. This trend is mostly because the average tax rate out of adjusted gross income has been increasing over time from 11.4 percent in 1960 to 13.6 percent in 1981. Therefore, the same percentage in taxes in 1960 and 1981 will give a smaller percentage change in disposable income in 1960 because taxes are smaller relative to income.

Expenditure-income responses. The disposable income and expenditure results can be combined to compute the aggregate marginal propensity to consume and the consumption income elasticity. These aggregate measures include the effects of both the increase in the level of aggregate income and the resulting shift in the distribution. Therefore they are the correct measures of the expenditure response to an aggregate income change if both the distribution model and the expenditure model are correct.

The aggregate marginal propensity to consume is calculated as the ratio of the level change in expenditures to the level change in disposable income. The expenditure-income elasticity is calculated as the ratio of the percentage change in aggregate expenditures to the percentage change in disposable income.

Table 5.6 shows the marginal propensities to consume computed using both approaches to the expenditure problem for three representative years. Two facts are striking. First, the calculated marginal propensities to consume are much higher in the expenditure ratio approach. Second, in both cases, the marginal propensities to consume decline over time. Again, this trend is probably due to the fact that incomes are rising over time. More higher-income consumer units lowers the aggregate marginal propensity to consume by giving more weight to the higher-income levels where the expenditure income responses are lower. The decline in marginal propensity

Table 5.6.   Estimated Aggregate Marginal
Propensities to Consume

	Expenditure Ratio Approach	Demand Equation Approach
1960	.65	.49
1970	.61	.38
1981	.59	.36

to consume under the expenditure ratio method is about 8 percent while in the demand equation approach the drop is 35 percent.

In the context of a macro model, the response of expenditures to income changes is very important in the properties of the model. For example, in a simple Keynesian framework, an autonomous income shock will change total income by the multiplier

$$dy = \frac{1}{(1 - c(1 - t))} da \tag{5.8}$$

where c = MPC and t is the tax rate. In this simple case, a higher MPC will result in a larger multiplier. Therefore, if either of the approaches to expenditures were incorporated into a macro model, the multiplier properties would likely change. However, the resulting differences in multipliers are difficult to predict because the actual multipliers are much more complicated than in the equation above. This simple multiplier does not include interest rate or supply effects.

The simple multiplier also includes a personal tax term which can be interpreted as the aggregate marginal tax rate which measures the tax leakage from the system. A higher marginal tax rate will reduce the multiplier by taking more income from consumers. Therefore, including the income distribution and a progressive tax structure in a macro model will probably reduce its multiplier.

Table 5.7 shows the expenditure-income elasticities, the same pattern as the marginal propensities shown in table 5.6. The expenditure ratio approach produces higher elasticities than the demand equation method and, in both cases, the elasticities decline as aggregate income rises. In

Table 5.7.   Estimated Aggregate
Expenditure-Income Elasticities

	Total Consumption	
	Expenditure Ratio Approach	Demand Equation Approach
1960	.69	.59
1970	.69	.43
1981	.67	.38

	Demand Equation Approach	
	Durables	Nondurables	Services
1960	.90	.43	.54
1970	.62	.37	.42
1981	.50	.37	.36

addition, table 5.7 shows the income elasticities for the three demand groups. As discussed above, durables have a greater income response than nondurables and services.

The marginal propensities to consume and the consumption-income elasticities are important because they summarize the response of expenditures to changes in income and can be used as a basis for comparison with results from other approaches. In this case the basic result is that the expenditure ratio method is more responsive to income changes than the demand equation approach. In order to judge if one might be more correct, other studies should be considered.

In comparing the expenditure-income responses in this model to results found in previous studies, two considerations are important. First, in the current model, there are no lagged income terms and therefore the entire direct impact of a change in income comes immediately. In other models, there are often lagged income terms which distinguish short- and long-range effects. Lagged income terms are not included in this model because they are not required in the theoretical derivation and because the cross section data used covers only one year.

The other important consideration is that the income responses presented here are static results and only indicate the direct income effects. For example, in the lift cycle consumption function, discussed below, a wealth term is included. Changes in income and savings will affect wealth which will have long-term impacts on consumption.

The expenditure-income responses in the current model can be compared with the results from two general classes of aggregate consumption functions. Broadly speaking, there are two basic forms of aggregate consumption functions in the literature. (This of course does not include simple Keynesian functions.) They are the functions which determine consumption using income and wealth as explanatory variables, such as the life cycle model, and functions which explain consumption using lagged income terms such as some permanent income models. Expenditure-income responses found in previous studies are compared with the current model below.

The basic form of a life cycle consumption function is

$$CE = a + b \cdot YD + c \cdot w \tag{5.9}$$

where w = wealth. In this case, the short-run MPC is the coefficient on disposable income. Typical estimates fall in the range 0.5–0.7, as advanced by Tobin and Dolde (1971). These short-run MPC's are consistent with observed APC's near 0.9 because of the wealth term. An MPC less than an

APC is a problem because it implies that over time, as income rises, the APC will fall. This has not been observed.

In this case, individuals consume out of current income and also wealth. Therefore the long-run APC can be less than the short-run MPC because another factor, wealth, also adds to consumption. In the short run, an increase in income will increase consumption and savings and the split will be determined by the MPC. However, over time, higher savings will result in higher wealth and therefore consumption will increase more than the original income change and MPC would indicate. By including terms other than income in the consumption function, the long-run APC can be greater than the short-run MPC.

Permanent-income-type consumption functions have income and lagged income terms as the major explanatory variables. For example,

$$CE = a + b_i\, YD + b_2\, YD_{-1}. \tag{5.10}$$

In the literature, expenditure-income responses of this general form have been presented in elasticity terms. A likely reason is that Friedman hypothesized that the permanent consumption-income elasticity is 1.0. Friedman also presented elasticity estimates from other studies which range from 0.76 to 0.9.

One way to look at the difference between the life cycle and permanent income forms is that the former uses a wealth term as a measure of long-run consumption planning and the latter uses lagged values of disposable income to measure permanent lifetime income. As discussed above, the long-run properties of the life cycle functions depend on changes in wealth and therefore cannot be directly computed from the consumption function. However, in the permanent income functions, income is the major factor and therefore both the short- and long-run consumption elasticities can be computed.

Expenditure ratio method. In the current model there are two estimates of the aggregate MPC. For the expenditure ratio approach to spending, the MPC is in the 0.6 range. This result compares well with the life cycle and some of the permanent income estimates in the literature for the short run. However, it is too low for a long-run expenditure-income response.

The long-run comparison is not obvious. As discussed above, the long-run observed APC close to 0.9 can be consistent with short-run MPCs of 0.5 to 0.7 in the life cycle model because of feedback to the wealth term. The question becomes, is there a corresponding term in the current model?

One possibility is the income distribution term. Recall from the demographic simulations that a shift in the distribution of disposable income affects expenditures by changing the weights on expenditures at the different income levels. This shift will also affect the aggregate MPC for the same reason. Therefore, the long-run MPC (and therefore the APC) may differ from the short-run MPC because of shifts in the income distribution. If an increase in income gives more income to lower income groups in the long-run, then the long-run MPC will exceed the static short-run estimate produced by the model.

Because the current system is only a model of taxes and expenditure with no feedback to the income distribution, possible long-run effects are not measured. Attempts were made to link the income distribution parameters with macro variables. However, no statistically significant results were obtained. Therefore, possible long-run expenditure income responses working through the income distribution cannot be tested.

Demand Equation Approach

In the demand equation approach, total expenditures increase by an average of 3.5 percent due to the income shock. The percentage increase declines from 4.4 percent in 1960 to 2.9 percent in 1981. As with the expenditure ratio approach, the likely explanation for this decline is that average income increases over the sample and shifts the distribution to the right. At higher incomes, the marginal propensities to consume decline less quickly than at lower income levels. Therefore, increases in aggregate income will have less of an impact on expenditures when the base income level is higher.

The computed expenditure-income responses are low when compared with previous results. The average MPC is 0.39 and the yearly values decline over time. By 1981, the MPC in this approach is 0.29. Both the average and the 1981 value are out of the 0.5 to 0.7 range found for the short-run MPC in the life cycle-type equations. Compared to the distributed lag income models, some studies have income elasticities in this range but only in the short run.

The increase in total expenditures in the demand equation approach is about 30 percent smaller than in the expenditure ratio method given the same change in income. This implies a smaller income response. For example, the marginal propensity to consume in 1970 is 0.378 in this case, compared with 0.608 in the expenditure ratio method.

The fact that the marginal propensities to consume decline less quickly at higher income levels can be seen by taking the second derivative of the demand equation. This measures the rate of change in the marginal propensity to consume as the income level changes.

$$d^2X_i/dYD_i^2 = -b/YD_i^2.$$ (5.11)

Because income enters this expression as the inverse of the square, as income rises the marginal propensity to consume declines more and more slowly. Therefore increases in income will increase expenditures less as the base income level rises. This pattern results in low aggregate responses to income changes.

The low income responses of the estimated semilog demand equations are unrealistic. Further simulations of the model using these equations, therefore, are likely to yield questionable results. Thus, the demand equation approach will be abandoned in favor of the expenditure ratio approach.

Other functional forms for the demand equations were considered in chapter 4. For example, a second-order polynomial was tried but was not used because the estimated parameters implied negative expenditures at high income levels. Further research in this area is needed.

Income Distribution Parameter Simulation

Assumptions

The first demographic simulation focuses on the impacts of alternative income distribution parameters. The simulation uses all of the historical simulation inputs with the exception of the alpha parameters in the gamma income distribution functions for both families and unrelated individuals. These parameters are increased by 10 percent over the base values.

Recall that the alpha parameter in a gamma density function controls the inequality of the distribution. To show this, the coefficient of variation of the gamma density is

$$c \cdot v = \sqrt{\alpha}$$ (5.12)

where α is the income distribution parameter. An increase in alpha reduces the coefficient of variation and therefore the inequality of the distribution. A 10 percent increase in alpha will reduce this statistic by roughly 5 percent. Therefore a 10 percent increase in both alpha parameters will give less weight to the tails of the distributions and more weight in the middle.

The expected results of the simulation are not obvious. On the cross section level, one would expect more income, taxes and expenditures in the middle-income range, and less in the extremes, because the increase in the alpha parameters causes more weight in the center of the distributions. However, a complicating factor is that the two income distributions, one for families and one for unrelated individuals, are combined into one distribution to compute taxes and expenditures. Thus, because the unrelated-individual distribution has a much lower mean, a shift toward the mean income in it could offset a similar shift in the family distribution. Fewer well-off unrelated individuals could offset a decrease in the number of low income families in the combined distribution. Therefore, although the impact of higher alpha parameters is predictable for both distributions alone, the outcome for the combined distribution cannot be determined analytically.

Results

The simulation results for the combined distribution show that there is an increase in the income in the middle income range, with decreases in the highest and lowest income brackets. This decrease in skewness is what would be expected from a single distribution given an increase in the alpha parameter. Although some offsetting may be present, the fact that families outweigh unrelated individuals, in both number and income, allows the combined results to be similar to a single distribution.

For before-tax income, increases in income in the middle-income range are exactly offset by the drops in income at the extremes of the distribution because total income is fixed. A shift in income from a high to a low level can be thought of as a reduction in the number of high-income persons and an increase in the number of those with lower incomes. The area under the density function does not change, but it becomes more centrally concentrated.

However, changes in taxes and expenditures at the different income levels are not offset in the aggregate because these variables depend upon the distribution of income. For example, a shift in income from a high to a low level will reduce taxes because the tax rates are lower at lower income levels. On the other hand, a shift in income from a low to a higher level will increase taxes, because the new tax rate will be higher. Therefore, this simulation could result in an increase or decrease in aggregate taxes because income is moved up from the lowest income levels and down from the highest. The result depends on weights from the income distribution. Aggregate taxes will drop if the upper level shifts dominate and fall if the changes in the low range dominate.

Aggregate expenditures react in the same way, but for different reasons. A shift in the distribution of income will change expenditures because the marginal propensity to consume varies with income level. An upward shift in the distribution will cause expenditures to fall because the marginal propensities to consume decline with income. This response is found in both

Table 5.8.   Summary of Income Distribution
Parameter Simulation Results

	Base Case	**Simulation**
Aggregate		
Personal Taxes (1972)	108.2	107.0
Personal Taxes (1981)	298.1	294.7
Real Disposable Income (1972)	823.1	824.4
Real Disposable Income (1981)	1045.2	1046.6
Total Expenditures (1972)	723.1	725.8
Total Expenditures (1981)	934.8	938.1
Cross Section		
Percentage of Income Above $25,000 (1972)	28.1	26.3
Percentage of Income Above $25,000 (1981)	28.5	26.9
Percentage of Income Below $3,000 (1972)	2.5	2.3
Percentage of Income Below $3,000 (1981)	2.9	2.6

approaches to expenditures. Conversely, a downward shift in the distribution will cause expenditures to increase. The aggregate result will depend on which shift dominates.

The aggregate results for the parameter simulation indicate that the changes in the upper income levels dominate. This outcome is to be expected because, for example, in the base case for 1981, 28.5 percent of income is reported in the above-$25,000 income interval and only 2.9 percent is in the under-$3,000 bracket. As a result of the high level dominance, taxes increased 1.12 percent in the simulation and all categories of expenditures fell.

In addition to the fact that the income shifting in the upper income groups dominates the aggregate results, this simulation has one other interesting outcome. The percentage change in taxes over the sample varies very little. This finding implies that the degree of progressivity in tax rates has been very stable because identical changes in the income distribution with fixed aggregate income produce very similar changes in the average tax rate. The average tax rate in any year is a weighted average of the effective tax rates at each income level where the weights are from the income distribution. An identical change in the weights resulting in very similar changes in average tax rates implies that the effective rates by income level are stable. This result is interesting given all of the changes in the tax laws over the years.

Consumer Makeup Simulation

This simulation tests the model's sensitivity to a shift in the income distribution in one direction without changing total income. The combined income distribution is shifted to the right by giving more weight to the higher-average-income family component and less weight to the lower-average-income unrelated individuals. Personal taxes increase because of the progressive tax rates and expenditures decrease because of the declining marginal propensities to consume. The results show how important these nonlinearities are to aggregate results due to an upward shift in the income distribution. Nonlinearities in cross section tax and expenditure functions are at the center of the redistribution problem.

The motivation for this simulation is that it shows the effects of a shift in the income distribution in a single direction without changing total income. The previous simulation altered the income distribution by making it more centrally weighted. Income moved in from the extreme income levels to the middle of the distribution and had offsetting effects on taxes and expenditures. The income multiplier simulation in the next section shifts the entire distribution upward, but also increases total income.

Assumptions

As a basis for the assumptions which give more weight to the family group of consumer units, this simulation fixes the ratio of persons living alone to total consumer units at the 1960 value. Over the historical period, the relative number of single-person consumer units has increased from 9.0 percent in 1960 to 20 percent in 1981. This has had the effect of limiting average consumer unit income because more consumer units — those living alone who would otherwise be living with family — are sharing the same level of aggregate income. This is not to say that families have lower incomes because of the increase in the relative number of persons living alone and that therefore they are worse off. It is possible that the increase in the relative number of unrelated individuals is a sign of a high income society which can afford more persons living alone.

The simulation fixes the ratio of single-person consumer units to all consumer units at the 1960 level. This assumption causes the number of families to be higher and the number of unrelated individuals to be lower than in the base case. In order to limit the changes in the simulation, aggregate income and the average incomes for the two groups — families and unrelated individuals — are held at the base values. This implies that the total number of consumer units is lower than in the base case. Given aggre-

Table 5.9.   Summary of Consumer Makeup Simulation Results

	Base Case	Simulation
Aggregate		
(Billions)		
Personal Taxes (1972)	108.2	107.5
Personal Taxes (1981)	298.1	295.1
Personal Social Security Taxes (1972)	26.1	26.3
Personal Social Security Taxes (1981)	111.1	112.6
Real Disposable Income (1972)	823.1	823.4
Real Disposable Income (1981)	1045.2	1046.4
Total Real Expenditures (1972)	723.1	724.6
Total Real Expenditures (1981)	934.8	937.3
Cross Section		
(Percentages)		
Percentage of Income Below $3,000 (1972)	2.5	2.4
Percentage of Income Below $3,000 (1981)	2.9	2.7
Percentage of Income Above $15,000 (1972)	57.6	57.0
Percentage of Income Above $15,000 (1981)	69.0	67.7

gate income and average income for the two consumer groups, fixing the ratio of the number of units in each group determines the total population.

Results

The combined distribution is shifted to the right by giving more weight to families with higher average incomes. For example, in 1981, the year with the largest difference, there are 8.3 percent more families with 8.3 percent more income than in the base. As an example of the impact on the combined income distribution, 69 percent of before-tax income falls above $15,000 (in 1972 dollars) in this simulation, compared with 67.7 percent in the base case. At the other end of the range, 6.0 percent of income falls below $5,000 (in 1972 dollars) compared with 7.5 percent in the base. At $12,000 the shift crosses over from declines in income to increases. However, although there are more higher-income families than in the base case, consumer unit average income is lower in the simulation as a result of the scenario assumptions. As a result, there is actually a drop in income in the above-$25,000 range offsetting the general rightward movement in the distribution. The same pattern occurs in other years, however the crossover point changes as the family group becomes more dominant compared with the base.

The increases in income at the higher income levels and the reductions at lower levels result in an increase in total taxes. Because tax rates increase with the level of income, shifting the distribution to the right will increase total taxes. In the low brackets, taxes fall because of the reduction in income in these brackets. However, these declines are offset by increases in taxes in higher brackets, because income moves from the lower levels to the higher, where the tax rates are greater. No income is lost; it moves to higher brackets.

As a result, personal federal taxes are higher than in the base case over the period with the greater differences in later years. By 1981, current dollar personal taxes were $7.6 billion, or 2.6 percent greater than the base case.

Contributions to social insurance also change as a result of the shift in the income distribution. However, unlike personal taxes, the social insurance tax is regressive because a taxpayer's contributions are based on wage income up to a legislated maximum. In this case, total contributions are lower because there are more consumer units above the maximum income.

The decrease in social security taxes is small, only $2.1 billion in 1981. This offsets the increase in personal federal taxes and feeds into the change in aggregate disposable income. Although the direction of the change in social security is correct, the magnitude is probably not reliable because of the problems with social security discussed in the estimation chapter above. Basically, the problem is that the model treats all personal income (except transfers) in the same way. For personal taxes, this is an acceptable assumption. However, because social security taxes are based on wage income only, this assumption causes problems. Not all personal income is taxed at the same rate, e.g., capital gains. However, this is taken into consideration by the effective tax rates, which are an average of all of the taxes on income at each income level. Additionally, because the maximum tax base was low until the mid 1970s, the errors in the income distribution at low income levels can cause large errors in social security collections.

The distribution of disposable income changes in the same way as the distribution of money income. However, the changes in the upper income brackets is smaller than in the before-tax case. In 1981, the simulation shows $28 billion (constant dollars) more in before-tax income in the highest income bracket and only $19 billion more in disposable income. In the low income levels, differences in the change in disposable income compared to before-tax income are much smaller because the tax rate is lower. Although the change in the distribution of before-tax income shifts money to higher brackets with no change in aggregate income, the resulting shift in disposable income gives a lower aggregate disposable income because of the progressive tax rates.

The aggregate results show that real disposable income is lower in the simulation and the reduction increases over the sample period. At the beginning of the period there is almost no change, because the major input into the simulation, the ratio of unrelated individuals to total consumer units, is very close to the base case. By 1981, when the percentage of families is 8.3 percent above the base, real disposable income is $2.5 billion, or 0.24 percent lower.

The expenditure results show that aggregate expenditures fall and that the model is very sensitive to the shift in the income distribution. The reduction in aggregate expenditures is due to the fact that the expenditure to disposable income ratios (which determine expenditures at each level of income) decline as income level rises and that the simulation causes a general upward shift in the distribution.

As a result, aggregate expenditures drop by $9.3 billion (constant dollars) in 1981 which is large when compared to the change in disposable income of only $2.5 billion. The major cause for this drop in expenditures must come from the shift in the income distribution and the declining expenditure to disposable income ratios. The change in disposable income can account for no more than $2.5 billion of the drop in expenditures because the marginal propensity to consume is less than 1.0 at all income levels. This limits the change in expenditures due to the change in disposable income to $2.5 billion. Therefore, most of the difference in expenditures must be a result of the nonlinear expenditure to disposable income relationship and the shift in the distribution of income.

Ten Percent Reduction in Tax Rates

This simulation reduces personal federal tax rates at all levels of income by 10 percent and results in a 10 percent reduction in aggregate taxes. The purpose of the simulation is to show the model's responses to a change in all tax rates by the same percentage. The simulation shows the effects of an across-the-board rate reduction similar to the Kemp-Roth tax cuts of 1981–1983. That tax reduction measure was intended to lower all marginal rates by 23.5 percent over a three year period as well as limit the highest marginal tax rate to 50 percent. This simulation will then be compared with the next which also reduces aggregate taxes by 10 percent, but does this by reducing tax rates of high-income consumers only.

In absolute terms, a percentage reduction in tax rates gives a larger benefit to higher income individuals because their tax rates and tax payments are higher. Thus, a 10 percent reduction in rates will result in a $50 benefit to the family paying $500 in taxes (roughly a $9,000 income in 1982) but $500 to the family with a $5,000 tax bill (about a $35,000 income).

In this simulation, all effective marginal tax rates are reduced by 10 percent. As one would expect, this results in lower aggregate taxes and higher personal expenditures and savings. The results of the simulation can be used to understand and judge the model's responses to this shock. This will be a basis for the policy simulations in the next chapter.

Aggregate Taxes and Disposable Income

Exactly as expected, aggregate personal federal taxes drop by 10 percent because all tax rates are reduced by 10 percent by assumption, and aggregate income is determined outside of the model. Reducing all effective marginal rates by the same percentage will cause all average rates by income level and in the aggregate to fall by the same percentage.

Aggregate disposable income increases by 1.3 percent on average over the sample period. This reflects the 10 percent tax reduction and is a smaller percentage change because taxes are roughly 12 percent of income. The percentage increase varies over the sample because the size of taxes relative to income varies from year to year.

Aggregate Expenditures and Savings

As expected, aggregate expenditures go up due to the 10 percent cut in tax rates because disposable income increases at all income levels. (As will be discussed below, the income effect dominates the substitution effect in the expenditure ratio approach.) The expenditure-disposable income responses are similar to those found in the income multiplier simulation, but differ somewhat in magnitude.

Total expenditures under the expenditure ratio method increase by an average of 1.1 percent, which implies an average sample period expenditure-disposable income elasticity of 0.82. This is slightly higher than the results from the income multiplier run. Table 5.10 shows the calculated expenditure-disposable income elasticities which result from the tax rate cut simulation for several years. These can be compared with the calculated elasticities from the income multiplier simulation shown in table 5.6.

Table 5.10.   Elasticities Computed in 10 Percent Tax Change
Simulation

	Expenditure Ratio Approach	Demand Equation Approach
1960	.85	.52
1970	.86	.35
1980	.82	.32

Inspection of the two tables shows that the calculated elasticities from the tax cut simulation are higher. The reason for this is that in the income multiplier simulation the income distribution is shifted toward higher income levels as a result of the higher level of aggregate income. Although the skewness of the distribution was fixed by assumption, all consumer units were moved upward on the income scale and as a result were shifted to lower MPC income levels. This gave increased weight to the low-spending, high-income consumers which kept the calculated aggregate expenditure income responses low.

In the current simulation, however, consumer units are not shifted on the income scale. Rather, their disposable incomes are increased through the tax cut. Therefore, less weight is given to low-spending, higher-income consumers than in the income multiplier run. As a result, the calculated income responses are higher in the tax cut simulation.

The expenditure responses due to a tax cut will differ depending on how taxes are changed. In this case, an across-the-board cut in rates gives a larger increase in disposable income to the higher income consumers both in absolute and relative terms, for reasons discussed above. If a tax reduction which results in similar aggregate revenue changes had been targeted to high-income individuals, the expenditure responses would be smaller. This response is examined in the next simulation.

Aggregate Savings

As a result of the 10 percent reduction in all tax rates, the level of personal savings increases. Savings increases because consumer units have more disposable income as a result of the tax cut and some of this increase in resources will go to private savings. The distinction between private and other savings is made because the increase in disposable income comes as a result of lower taxes. Unless the government also reduces its expenditures, government savings will decline. The concept of total savings is discussed further in chapter 6.

Real savings increase by an average of 30 percent of the increase in disposable income. This reflects an aggregate marginal propensity to consume of 70 percent given an across-the-board tax rate reduction. Therefore, the model predicts that a 10 percent cut in tax rates in 1972 would have resulted in a first-round increase in savings of $2.9 billion or 2.9 percent.

Cross Section Taxes and Disposable Income

As in the aggregate, personal federal taxes drop in all cross section income brackets by 10 percent, a direct result of the assumed shock. For low-

Table 5.11.   Summary of Results for 10 Percent Tax Cut

	Base	**Simulation**
Summary of Simulation Results		
Aggregate		
(Billions)		
Personal Taxes (1972)	108.2	97.4
Personal Taxes (1981)	298.1	268.3
Real Disposable Income (1972)	823.1	834.0
Real Disposable Income (1981)	1045.2	1060.0
Total Real Expenditures (1972)	723.1	731.2
Total Real Expenditures (1981)	934.8	946.2
Cross Section		
(Percentages)		
Percentage of Disposable Income Above $25,000 (1972)	24.7	24.9
Percentage of Disposable Income Above $25,000 (1981)	26.8	27.1
Percentage of Disposable Income Below $3,000 (1972)	2.9	2.9
Percentage of Disposable Income Below $3,000 (1981)	3.4	3.4

income consumer units which pay almost no taxes in the base case, this amounts to almost no change in disposable income. As income levels rise, the 10 percent cut in tax rates results in a larger relative change in disposable income. For example, in 1972, disposable income increased by only 0.03 percent in the first income cell, and by 2.1 percent in the top interval, showing that an across-the-board percentage rate reduction benefits higher income individuals.

Tax Rate Reduction for High Income Taxpayers Simulation

This simulation reduces tax rates in the upper income brackets only such that aggregate taxes fall by 10 percent. In the aggregate, the shock in this simulation is identical to the previous across-the-board rate reduction in that aggregate taxes are reduced by 10 percent. However, because the benefits are targeted at high income brackets, the changes in aggregate expenditures and savings are likely to be different. Based on the previous sensitivity simulations, this simulation should result in smaller increases in aggregate expenditures and larger increases in savings compared with the 10 percent

Table 5.12. Summary of Results for High Income Tax Cut Simulation

	Base	Simulation
Aggregate		
(Billions)		
Personal Taxes (1972)	108.2	97.4
Personal Taxes (1981)	298.1	268.3
Real Disposable Income (1972)	823.1	834.0
Real Disposable Income (1981)	1045.2	1060.6
Total Real Expenditures (1972)	723.1	730.2
Total Real Expenditures (1981)	934.8	945.1
Cross Section		
(Percentages)		
Percentage of Disposable Income Above		
$25,000 (1972)	24.7	25.7
Percentage of Disposable Income Above		
$25,000 (1981)	26.8	26.7
Percentage of Disposable Income Below		
$3,000 (1972)	2.9	2.9
Percentage of Disposable Income Below		
$3,000 (1981)	3.4	3.4

across-the-board tax rate reduction simulation. The reason for this is that higher-income consumer units spend less and save more of a given increase in disposable income. Therefore, a tax cut benefiting high-income consumers will result in greater additional savings.

The purpose of this simulation is, together with the previous run, to show how aggregate shocks of the same dollar amount but targeted at different income levels, give different results. Together, the two simulations show the results of the cross section consumption functions responding to tax rate changes at different income levels. This comparison forms part of the basis for the tax policy simulations in the next chapter. This sensitivity simulation shows that the model does produce reasonable results given a redistribution of tax rates.

Assumptions

The simulation reduces tax rates paid by the upper-income consumer units such that aggregate taxes fall by 10 percent. To do this, tax rates in the brackets above $25,000 are all reduced by the same amount. The percentage point reduction varies from year to year over the simulation period, because the amount of income earned above $25,000 relative to aggregate income varies over time. In the base case, 28 percent of adjusted gross income is earned by consumer units with incomes above $25,000 in 1972. By 1981, 70 percent of income is above $25,000 in the base case. These figures represent percentages of income and not consumer units. The reason for the dramatic shift is that these figures are reported in nominal terms, and prices almost doubled over the period. Only a small part of the shift is due to growth in real income per consumer unit, which increased only 3 percent from 1972 to 1981.

The shock is implemented slightly differently from the previous simulation for convenience. Rather than change the tax rates in each bracket by the same percentage, this run reduces the upper-bracket rates by the same percentage point amount. In this case, the percentage changes in taxes compared with the base case will decrease in the highest brackets rather than remain constant as in the previous run.

Of the three general categories of tax cuts—fixed percentage, fixed percentage point, and equal amount of tax reduction—a fixed percentage point tax cut would be in the middle of a fairness scale if it were given to all taxpayers. Although high-bracket consumers receive a larger tax cut, it would be smaller in percentage terms than for a lower-income individual.

Reducing tax rates by a fixed percentage point makes this simulation not directly comparable with the previous run. Had the tax cut been given to the upper brackets by the fixed percentage method, more of the tax reduction would have gone to the highest-income consumers. This would have made the difference in expenditures and saving between the two 10 percent tax cut runs greater.

Aggregate Taxes and Disposable Income

By construction, aggregate taxes fall by 10 percent, exactly as in the previous run. As a result, aggregate disposable income also changes in the same way as the previous simulation, a 1.3 percent average increase over the sample.

Aggregate Expenditures

Aggregate expenditures increase as a result of the tax cut for upper-income individuals, but by less than in the across-the-board tax rate reduction case. The differences in expenditures are larger in the earlier years of the simulation when the tax cuts are concentrated on fewer high-income consumers. In the later years, when inflation pushes more consumer units above the $25,000 income level, the results of this simulation become closer to the across-the-board run. This pattern occurs in both approaches to expenditures.

Total expenditures increase by 0.95 percent on average over the period 1972 through 1981. This is somewhat less than the 1.1 percent increase in total expenditures observed in the previous simulation where all tax rates were reduced. The difference is due to the fact that, in the model, higher income consumer units spend a smaller proportion of additional income and in this run all of the tax cut goes to high-income consumers. Therefore, aggregate expenditures increase less in the current simulation.

The difference between the two 10 percent aggregate tax cut simulations is greater in the first years of the simulation because the tax cut goes to fewer consumers in the current run. As mentioned above, the shock in this run reduces taxes for consumers with incomes above $25,000 in nominal terms. In 1972, the base case shows 28 percent of income above $25,000 and in 1981 this grows to 70 percent due to inflation. Thus, in 1972, the tax cut is given to only a few consumers with relatively high incomes. By 1981, more consumer units benefit from the tax cut and the current simulation is much more like the tax cut for all consumers. Therefore, compared with the across-the-board tax rate reduction simulation, expenditures in the current case increase by $0.8 billion less in 1972, and only $0.1 billion less in 1981. This result has significant implications for savings, which are discussed below.

Aggregate Savings

Compared with the base case, aggregate real savings increase due to the tax cut. The level of real savings goes up by an average of $4.2 billion over the period 1972 through 1981. This is $0.6 billion more than the average increase due to the across-the-board rate cut. Because in the current simulation the tax cut benefits relatively fewer consumer units in the early years of the period, savings increases by $0.8 billion more in 1972 but only $0.1 billion more in 1981 than in the all-consumer tax cut case. Thus, a tax rate change targeted at upper-income consumers will have a greater impact on savings than a change of equal aggregate magnitude affecting all consumers. The fewer the high-income consumers who benefit from the tax cut, the smaller will be the savings increase.

Cross Section Results

The cross section results show that the shock to the model directly affects only the upper-income consumer units. In general, taxes decrease and expenditures increase in the upper-income intervals. However, because the tax cut is given to consumer units with incomes above $25,000 in nominal terms, and the cross section expenditures are reported in brackets in real terms, changes are observed in the middle income range as well by the end of the simulation period. The $25,000 nominal income level above which tax cuts are given translates to about a $12,000 real income level by 1981.

Taxes. By assumption, there are no changes in taxes for consumer units with incomes under $25,000 in nominal terms. For those with higher incomes, taxes are lower. The rate reduction for all those with incomes above $25,000 is about 6 percentage points in 1972, but is only 4 points in 1981. The reason for this is that a greater percentage of income falls above the $25,000 point in 1981 due to inflation, and therefore a smaller rate reduction is necessary to lower aggregate taxes by 10 percent.

The simulation assumes that all rates for those affected are reduced by the same percentage point amount. This results in a greater percentage reduction in taxes for those closer to the $25,000 mark, and lower for the highest income taxpayers. In 1972, taxes in the $25–30,000 bracket are reduced by 42 percent while taxes of those with incomes above $50,000 are 3 percent lower.

Expenditures. Expenditures increase in the upper-income range as a result of the tax cut. In 1972, all of the increase in expenditures comes in the twelfth income cell, above $25,000. However, because the cross section expenditures are reported in constant dollars, changes show up in lower brackets in later years. By 1981, some of the consumer units in the ninth income bracket, $12,000 to $15,000 are affected by the change.

A slight problem with the model is that the after-tax rate of return, which models the substitution effect between current and future consumption, changes for all consumer units even though the actual rate of return for lower- and middle-income consumers should not change in this case. The problem is that, in estimation, the after-tax rate of return is included as a time series effect and, as a result, only the aggregate average tax rate appears in the expenditure functions. In this simulation the aggregate average tax rate decreases by 10 percent and therefore expenditures under the expenditure ratio method are affected. However, the impact is very small, $0.17 billion or 0.02 percent of total expenditures in 1972, indicating that in the model the income effect dominates the substitution effect.

Redistribution of Tax Rates Simulation

This simulation redistributes the personal federal tax burden from high-income to low- and middle-income consumer units while trying to maintain

Table 5.13.   Summary of Results for Tax Shift Simulation

	Base	Simulation
Aggregate		
(Billions)		
Personal Taxes (1972)	108.2	112.0
Personal Taxes (1981)	298.1	292.9
Real Disposable Income (1972)	823.1	819.3
Real Disposable Income (1981)	1045.2	1047.9
Total Real Expenditures (1972)	723.1	719.7
Total Real Expenditures (1981)	934.8	935.6
Cross Section		
(Percentages)		
Percentage of Disposable Income Above $25,000 (1972)	24.7	25.6
Percentage of Disposable Income Above $25,000 (1981)	26.8	27.5
Percentage of Disposable Income Below $3,000 (1972)	2.9	2.9
Percentage of Disposable Income Below $3,000 (1981)	3.4	3.4

the base level of aggregate taxes. The purpose of the simulation is to test and understand the model's responses to a redistribution of taxes. The redistribution of taxes is similar to what would happen under a flat-tax system which is considered in the next chapter.

Based on the previous sensitivity simulations, shifting taxes from upper- to middle- and low-income consumer units should reduce aggregate expenditures and, assuming fixed disposable income, increase savings. The reason for this is that the tax shift moves disposable income from high-spending lower-income consumers to lower-spending high-income consumers.

Assumptions

The simulation increases the marginal tax rates of low- and middle-income consumers by 10 percent and reduces the marginal rates of higher-income units by approximately 20 percent. The marginal rates of this upper group are reduced by a greater percentage to offset the increases in rates in the lower-income levels. Had the reduction been 10 percent, average rates in the first few high-income brackets would have been higher than the base case because of the increases in the lower-level rates. Recall that the average rate in any bracket is built up from the marginal rates in lower brackets. In addition, a few marginal rates in the upper brackets were changed by different amounts to ensure that the average rates never decline as income rises. This is done to make the scenario more plausible.

The crossover point — the income level below which rates are increased and above which rates are decreased — varies over the sample period. The point is chosen to be approximately twice average income in each year of the sample. However, because the tax brackets are intervals, the crossover point does not follow this rule exactly.

Taxes and Disposable Income

Although the simulation attempts to shift the tax rates with no effect on aggregate taxes, the arbitrary rate changes and crossover points chosen do not accomplish this exactly. However, the resulting aggregate taxes are close to the base case in some years. Although taxes could have been made to match the base exactly, it is not done because the differences in taxes and also disposable income in other years show interesting results and these are discussed below.

Aggregate taxes are close to the base case in three years — less than a 0.4 percent error in 1973, 1978, and 1980. In these years, aggregate disposable income is less than 0.05 percent different from the base. The largest differences in taxes occur in 1972 and 1976 and these result in aggregate disposable income differences of 0.5 percent.

The tax shift causes disposable income to fall in lower-income classes and increase in the top ones. Because the crossover point for the tax rate changes is close to $25,000 in real terms, most of the increase is in the highest income interval.

Expenditures

Aggregate total consumer spending drops in all but two years, when disposable income increases by $2.7 and $5.4 billion respectively. The higher levels of disposable income are due to the fact that the tax rate shock is not chosen perfectly. However, in the two other years when disposable income also is higher than the base case, expenditures fall. These reductions must be due to the redistribution of taxes from high- to low-income consumers. In a more traditional model without cross section expenditure functions, expenditures probably would increase given an increase in disposable income.

In the years in which changes in aggregate taxes are the smallest, there is a 0.03 percent decrease in disposable income and a 0.1 percent drop in total expenditures. The spending drops are also due to cross section effects and this idea can be confirmed by looking at the cross section results. Using 1973 as an example, because aggregate disposable income is almost the same as in the base case, expenditures decline for those with incomes under $25,000 in 1972 dollars by $3.5 billion. This is a result of a $3.9 billion decline in disposable income for the same group and implies a group marginal propensity to consume of 0.89. In the same year, high-income consumer units' disposable income increases by $3.8 billion as a result of the tax shift, and this group increases expenditures by $2.5 billion. This yields an MPC of 0.66. The difference in the expenditure changes and MPCs of the two groups shows that a shift in taxes from high- to lower-income consumers which does not change aggregate disposable income will result in a drop in aggregate expenditures. The tax shift causes a redistribution of disposable income in favor of lower-MPC consumers. Therefore aggregate spending falls and, because disposable income does not change, savings increases. This is discussed below.

Because individual MPCs decline as income rises, the arbitrary choice of the crossover point will not affect the direction of the expenditure changes. However, the simulation shows that as the crossover point declines in real terms, the expenditure shifts also decline. With fixed aggregate income, any shift in taxes from high- to low-income consumers will cause expenditures to decline and therefore savings to increase. In addition, the results from years in which aggregate disposable income increases and expenditures fall show that the fixed aggregate income condition is not necessary.

Summary

This chapter first shows how different parts of the model — income distribution, tax rates, and expenditures — fit together. In doing so, the more questionable assumptions such as the pooling of unrelated individuals and families into one group of consumer units, the treatment of transfer payments, and the computation of contributions to Social Security based on all income rather than just wage income are discussed.

The historical simulation shows that the major aggregate variables, personal federal taxes and expenditures, follow history well. Aggregate taxes, however, have a small overcollection bias in all but one year. To correct for this, all tax rates are adjusted by the same percentage so that taxes are predicted correctly. This proves to be of cosmetic value only.

On the cross section level, disposable income and expenditures are compared with history in share of aggregate form for 1972. Although mostly discussed in chapter 4, the share of aggregates in each income interval have small relative errors in the middle-income range, and larger errors at low- and high-income levels. This pattern holds true for disposable income and all of the expenditure categories. Although this comparison is made for only one year, it is informative. The relatively large errors in the key cross section variables, especially in the high income intervals, suggest that the model should not be used to study the specific changes in any one income interval.

However, when the twelve income intervals are collapsed into three broad ranges, the errors in the key variables are much smaller. In this way the model can be used to study general cross section impacts as well as aggregate results.

Three types of multiplier experiments are presented. The first two are demographic in nature in that they test the model's sensitivity to changes in the income distribution parameters and the mix of families and unrelated individuals. The third multiplier run increases aggregate income by 10 percent. This run shows the responses in taxes and expenditures to an income change and can be used to compute aggregate marginal propensities to consume and expenditure-income elasticities. Finally, three tax-rate simulations are discussed.

The first demographic simulation increases the alpha parameters of the family and unrelated individual income distributions by 10 percent. Recall that an increase in the alpha parameter of a gamma distribution increases income inequality. Therefore, in this simulation, the distribution of before-tax income is more centrally weighted with a greater percentage of the consumer units having income closer to the mean. For taxes, the shift in consumer units from low to middle incomes increases collections because the rates are progressive. However, this is outweighed by the decline in taxes due to the movement from high- to middle-incomes. This occurs because there are more consumer units with more income in the high brackets.

The pattern for expenditures is the same but of opposite sign. Despite the fact that disposable income falls, aggregate expenditures increase. Because average propensities to consume fall as incomes rise, the shift from high- to middle-income consumer units increases expenditures. This is offset to some degree by the drop in spending due to the upward movement of some low income persons.

The important conclusion from this simulation is that, although the results do change when the distribution parameters are increased, the impact on key aggregate variables is small. Therefore errors in the estimated distribution parameters are not likely to have a large effect on the tax structure simulation results in the next chapter.

The second demographic simulation changes the mix of consumer units by increasing the number of families and reducing the number of unrelated individuals. Aggregate income is fixed at base levels. Because families have higher incomes, this simulation shifts the distribution of income toward higher levels. The aggregate results are higher taxes and lower expenditures because of the nonlinearities in the tax and expenditure equations.

The simulation offers two major insights into the model. First, it shows the different properties of the expenditure methods. For the same shift in the distribution of disposable income, expenditures decrease less under the expenditure ratio method than under the demand equation approach. This, along with a similar result in the income multiplier run, indicates that the marginal propensities to consume decrease less quickly as income rises in the expenditure ratio approach. Therefore, shifts in the distribution of disposable income will affect expenditures under the demand equation approach more than under the expenditure ratio method.

The second insight from this simulation is that in this model the mix of families and unrelated individuals matters. However, changing the mix only affects the results by changing the shape of the combined income distribution because of the simplifying assumption that families and unrelated individuals are added together into one type of consumer. A priori, one would expect that these two groups would make spending decisions differently. Therefore, although more linkages would be desirable, the demographic breakdown of consumer units still affects results.

Next is a simulation in which aggregate income is increased by 10 percent. This run is important because it is the basis for computing the income responses of taxes and expenditures. These measures cannot be derived analytically because they depend on the income distribution. Therefore a simulation is necessary. The tax-income response shows that personal federal taxes increase by 15.7 percent for a 10 percent increase in income. This is very close to the 15 percent increase in taxes for the same income shock found by Pechman (1977).

Finally, three tax rate simulations are presented as background for the tax policy scenarios in the next chapter. The first is a 10 percent reduction in all marginal tax rates which results in a 10 percent drop in aggregate taxes. This shock causes expenditures at all income levels to increase. The resulting changes in aggregate disposable income and expenditures yield an average expenditure elasticity of 0.82 which is higher than the same elasticity found in the income multiplier run. This is because the tax cut increases disposable income at all income levels without shifting the income distribution.

The second tax simulation also reduces aggregate taxes by 10 percent, but by reducing rates for only high-income taxpayers. The simulation shows that an equal tax cut in the aggregate can yield different changes in expenditures and savings if it is targeted at different income groups. In general, an alternative tax policy directed at those with high incomes will have a smaller expenditure impact and a greater savings impact given equal changes in disposable income.

The third tax sensitivity run redistributes taxes from high- to low-income consumers while attempting to maintain the base levels of aggregate tax collections. This simulation shows how such a redistribution, which is similar to the flat tax policy scenario in the next chapter, affects expenditures and savings. The simulation shows that, when aggregate disposable income is close to the base case, reductions in low-income consumers' expenditures due to higher taxes might not be offset by increased spending by the high-income consumers who benefit from the tax redistribution. The end result will depend on the levels of income at which tax rates are increased and decreased. Therefore, a redistribution of taxes with no aggregate tax impact can alter aggregate spending and savings.

Conclusion

The purpose of this chapter has been to explain how the model fits together and how it performs over history in order to answer the question "Can the model be used to study a restructuring of federal taxes, and can the results be believed?"

By design, the model can be used to study the direct impact of a restructured federal tax law on expenditures. Because personal taxes and expenditures are simulated over the income distribution, tax rates can be changed at different income levels and the impacts on expenditures can be seen. One problem, however, is that effective tax rates which include reductions due to deductions and exemptions are used. In addition, the effective rates include all types of taxpayers and do not distinguish tax rates by marital status. Therefore, scenarios which involve changes in deductions, exemptions and tax rates by marital status cannot be directly studied.

The question of model performance can be addressed in two ways. First, does the model fit the historical data, and second, are the multiplier properties reasonable? These questions are addressed for each part of the model below.

In chapter 4, the income distributions approximated by the gamma density function were shown to have large errors in the small income intervals in the tails of the distributions. These errors might have been smaller if a different density function had been used. However, the gamma was chosen because its two parameters are easily interpreted in economic terms. The alpha parameter alone controls skewness and the beta parameter controls scale. This is especially important in a long-term study in which there are large changes in prices and nominal income levels.

Personal federal taxes are the joint result of the estimated income distribution and the effective tax rates. Without adjustments, aggregate taxes are predicted over history with an average error of 5 percent. This is a good result considering that taxes are constructed using the income distribution and effective rates which come from different data sources.

In addition, taxes also respond to an income shock in a reasonable way. Given a 10 percent increase in aggregate income, personal taxes increase by 15.7 percent. This is similar to a response in taxes found by Pechman (1977).

On a cross section basis, however, the tax results are questionable because the income distribution has errors in the narrowly defined income intervals and these errors are passed along to tax collections. Therefore, results based on changes in narrowly defined tax brackets should be taken cautiously.

Expenditures are predicted in two ways and the methods can be distinguished by the cross section expenditure equations. The expenditure ratio method computes spending at each income level based on the ratio of expenditures to disposable income in the 1972 Consumer Expenditure Survey. Under this approach, aggregate predicted expenditures fit historical data closely. In addition, the short-run expenditure-income responses fall within previously accepted ranges. That the aggregate results fit the historical data implies that long-run properties are also within accepted bounds. However, long-run response cannot be determined directly because of possible feedback through the income distribution. This link is similar to life cycle equations which measure short-run MPCs directly, but long-run impacts indirectly through changes in wealth. Attempts to link the income distribution parameters with macro variables failed.

Expenditures are also determined by simulating semilog demand equations over the income distribution. These results also fit the data well in the aggregate. However, when the aggregate MPCs are computed, they fall below previously accepted ranges. Although the good fit in the aggregate over history implies accepted long-run properties, the low short-run MPCs cast doubt on the usefulness of the demand equation approach. Therefore, because of the unreasonably low income responses, the demand equation method is not used in policy simulations in chapter 6. The demand equation method is left as an area for future research.

A final basis on which to judge a new consumption sector are the observations on consumption made by Kuznets (1946) and summarized by Branson (1972). These observations lead to the rejection of a simple Keynesian consumption function and the development of the life cycle and permanent income theories. The observations are (1) In cross section, MPCs decline as income rises; (2) Over the business cycle, the average consumption rate is below average at the peak and above in the trough. As income fluctuates, the MPC is below the APC; (3) Long-run aggregate data show a steady average consumption rate. Therefore, in the aggregate, the MPC is equal to the APC in the long-run.

The demand equation approach to expenditures considered here is able to explain these three observations. By design, the model is able to handle variable MPCs in the cross section. This property, and progressive tax rates, are the main reasons why expenditures are determined by simulation over the income distribution.

The second observation, that the aggregate APC is counter-cyclic, seems to be supported by the base simulation. In the high-growth years of the mid 1960s and late 1970s the average consumption rates are below the decade averages. In the trough years 1970 and 1974, the average rates are above the decade average.

The last observation, that the aggregate APC is stable over time, is supported by the model. The predicted APC averages 0.89 and is stable over the historical simulation.

6

Economic Impact of
Two Flat Tax Rate Structures

Introduction

This chapter presents simulations of two alternative personal federal tax rate structures, a flat tax and the Bradley-Gephardt proposal. In addition, recent developments in personal federal taxes are discussed. The income distribution and expenditure model is used to simulate the effects of the two alternative tax structures on personal savings and expenditures. In addition, the flat tax is also simulated in conjunction with the Wharton Long-Term model to account for the feedback effects of changes in savings and personal spending on macroeconomic variables, especially investment.

Results from the income distribution and expenditure model are based on the expenditure ratio method only. The demand equation method is not discussed because of the questionable properties observed in the multiplier simulations. The low responses of aggregate expenditures to income changes cast doubt on simulation results using the demand equation approach. Therefore only the expenditure ratio method is used.

The campaign and election of Ronald Reagan to the presidency in 1980 focused attention on alternative personal federal tax structures as a way of increasing personal savings. Higher levels of personal savings were thought to be one means of increasing private investment. Higher levels of private investment would lead to increased productivity, higher output, and lower inflation.

Both before and after the 1980 election, Reagan supported a tax reduction proposed by Senator William Roth and Representative Jack Kemp which called for a 30 percent decrease in all personal tax rates over a three year period. The Kemp-Roth proposal was incorporated in the Economic Recovery Tax Act (ERTA) of 1981 which, along with other measures, reduced all personal tax rates by 23.5 percent over three years beginning in 1981.

In addition, Reagan has supported the idea of a flat tax—a system under which all taxpayers would be subject to the same tax rate regardless of income level.

Another alternative tax system has been suggested by Senator William Bradley and Representative Richard Gephardt. Under their proposal, tax rates would remain progressive, but the maximum marginal rate would be limited to 30 percent. In addition, the number of tax brackets would be greatly reduced, and many deductions to taxable income eliminated. The Bradley-Gephardt proposal is also discussed.

Recent Developments in Tax Policy

The Kemp-Roth tax cuts supported by President Reagan were intended to improve the economy by stimulating the supply of goods and services. More traditional public economists might suggest that personal tax cuts increase economic activity through higher consumer demand, especially when high unemployment indicates a lack of aggregate demand. The Kemp-Roth program, however, was supported on the idea that lower personal tax rates would lead to increased personal savings and labor supply. Higher levels of savings and labor were intended to increase the two main inputs to production, capital and labor, and thus lower production costs. Workers would be willing to supply more labor at the same before-tax wage—the same employer cost—because their after-tax wage increased. The capital stock would be increased because there would be more funds available from private savings for investment. Therefore, by cutting personal taxes, increased incentives to save and work would result in more output produced at given prices.

In addition to higher economic growth, some suggested that the Kemp-Roth plan would lead to increases in tax collections. As a result of the tax cuts, personal income would increase by a greater percentage than the tax rates were reduced, and tax collections would actually go up. This idea is represented by the Laffer curve, which holds that tax revenues can be increased by reducing tax rates if the original rates are above a critical level. There is no agreement on the existence of the Laffer curve or the critical tax rate. For a review of this, see Nariman Behravesh (1980).

Other calls for lower taxes have been based on the notion that the federal government has grown too large. (Feldstein and Feenberg (1983) consider other tax incentives to increase savings using simulation techniques.) This is a political philosophy rather than an economic issue. Reducing taxes would force a reduction in the size of government—or at least check its growth by limiting revenues to be spent. However, reduced growth in federal revenues in the past three years has not limited spending in real or current dollar terms to the same extent, and the federal deficit has grown.

The Kemp-Roth proposal became the Economic Recovery Tax Act (ERTA) of 1981. Among its measures ERTA reduced all personal federal tax rates by 23.5 percent over a three year period. The tax cuts are called "across-the-board" because all rates were reduced by the same percentage. High-income taxpayers received a greater absolute reduction than did those with low incomes.

The macroeconomic impact of the ERTA personal tax reductions, however, cannot be determined by observing what has happened since the program was passed into law. Macroeconomics does not have controlled experiments and many factors can vary. At the same time as the first ERTA tax cuts were given to consumers, the last quarter of 1981, real GNP declined by 5.3 percent on an annual basis. Many economists blame this drop in real GNP not on the tax cuts but on high interest rates caused by restrictive monetary policy. Some argue that high interest rates were caused by fears of large deficits brought on by tax cuts without corresponding spending reductions. Any positive effects of the tax cuts were shadowed by the GNP decline. In fact, the tax cuts may have softened the negative effects of the tight monetary policy.

Econometric models can of course be used to isolate the effects of changes in a set of exogenous variables. In a multiplier simulation of the income distribution and expenditure model alone, a 10 percent decrease in tax rates resulted in personal expenditures increasing by 1.1 percent and the level of savings increasing by 3.0 percent in one sample year, 1972. The simulation did not include feedback effects from the macro economy.

In a complete macro model simulation, the Wharton Long-Term model (1981) indicates that tax cuts increase economic growth by stimulating consumer demand. (The complete simulation result has been deleted and only illustrative results are available.) A simulation completed in 1981 studied the effects of eliminating the third phase of the ERTA personal tax cuts. Imposing the third 10 percent tax cut increased average real GNP growth by 0.4 percentage points over the period 1983 through 1987 and pushed up the federal deficit by $40 billion in 1984.

The Wharton model did not show any significant supply-side effects. The personal savings rate increased in the short run because of the lagged response of consumption to changes in disposable income in the Wharton Long-Term model. However, there was little impact on interest rates, the mechanism through which higher personal savings stimulates investment. Labor supply increased by only 10,000 workers after four years of the tax cut.

Theoretical Links between Tax Rates and Savings

This section reviews the theoretical links between personal federal tax rates and individual savings and labor supply decisions. Attention is given to expenditures and savings because they directly affect investment and the macro economy.

In chapter 2 the theory of the consumer and the mechanisms through which taxes affect personal spending and savings were presented. For individual consumer units, there are two channels, the direct changes to disposable income and the income and substitution effects which are due to the change in the after-tax rate of substitution between current and future consumption.

First, a change in tax rates affects the consumer's disposable income directly. A decrease in rates allows the consumer to spend more now and also save more for future consumption. This effect corresponds to the disposable income term in a consumption function. As long as the consumer's marginal propensity to consume is between 0.0 and 1.0, an increase in disposable income will allow both expenditures and savings to go up. The consumer's actual response, however, depends on other factors as well.

At the same time, reduced tax rates alter the after-tax rate of substitution of present for future consumption. This corresponds to the interest rate (or intertemporal price) term in a consumption function and has two effects. On the one hand, it reduces the price of future consumption in terms of present goods and therefore is an incentive to save. This is the substitution effect.

On the other hand, a higher after-tax rate of return raises a consumer's investment income. Therefore, to meet a given future consumption goal, the consumer needs to save a smaller share of his income. Through the income effect, a reduction in tax rates implies a possible reduction in savings.

A change in tax rates has an indeterminant effect on an individual's expenditure and savings decisions. If the income effect dominates, the interest rate term will be positive (lower tax rates yield lower savings) and if the substitution effect is stronger, the interest rate coefficient will be negative (lower tax rates yield higher savings).

Current tax laws make the situation more complicated because interest costs — the result of being a net borrower — are a tax deduction for those who itemize deductions. (This argument assumes that the yield from tax free bonds is determined by marginal tax rates. If tax rates are reduced, tax free yields will increase to maintain equal rates of return for similar risk bonds. The argument ignores special retirement plans such as individual retirement accounts.) Thus, a tax rate reduction for a taxpayer who itemizes deductions will increase the actual cost of borrowing for current consumption, making current consumption more expensive with respect to future consumption. For net savers, interest income is taxed, and a lower tax rate will result in a substitution effect toward more savings. For those who can deduct interest payments from their tax base, the tax law is symmetric in that it treats interest payments and income consistently.

However, if interest payments are not deductible—the case for about two-thirds of all tax returns in 1981—a change in tax rates will have no substitution effect on borrowing for current consumption. Thus, lowering tax rates will not encourage more savings through the substitution effect for net borrowers who do not itemize.

The income effect of a change in tax rates for a net borrower also depends on the consumer's method of determining deductions. As in the substitution effect case, there is no income effect for a consumer who does not itemize deductions, because taxes only affect the cost of borrowing if interest payments are deducted. For those who do itemize, the cost of current versus future consumption will increase if tax rates are reduced. Therefore, both current spending and savings will fall (not increase) due to the income effect, because lifetime income falls.

The claim made by some supporters of tax reform—that reduced tax rates will increase savings—is based on the assumption that the substitution effect of higher after-tax rates of return outweighs the pure income effect of more resources as a result of the change in the after-tax rate of return. Economic theory cannot answer this question and empirical evidence is required.

In chapter 2, past evidence on the dominance of the income or substitution effect is reviewed. For example, Boskin estimates a negative interest rate term in an aggregate consumption function for the U.S. economy. This indicates a stronger substitution effect. But Howrey and Hymans criticize this finding, and in repeating the analysis, find the result not robust. They also review other studies and conclude that there is no strong evidence for the dominance of either the income or substitution effect.

One possible reason for this is that the theory discussed above describes the behavior of individuals and most empirical studies are based on observed aggregate data. However, the question of whether the income or substitution effect dominates—the question of the sign of the rate-of-return term—depends on individual consumers. Studies using aggregate data fail to take the distribution of income and the progressive tax structure into account by making the representative consumer assumption. As a result, the aggregate average tax rate, which is lower than the marginal tax rates for almost all consumers, is used. Therefore, it is not surprising that there are no definitive aggregate results.

Tax Rate Links to Savings in the Model

Ideally, the cross section expenditure equation should include an after-tax rate of return term where the tax rate is the marginal tax rate. At the cross-sectional level the marginal rate used can correspond to income level and thus the after-tax rate of return can be correctly specified. An after-tax rate of return variable was tried in the cross section equations. The interest rate component was of course fixed because the cross-sectional sample was taken in one time period. Therefore, the variation in the after-tax rate of return variable came from tax rates increasing with income in the cross section. Estimation did not produce a coefficient significantly different from zero using several different functional forms. This result is not surprising for several reasons, including that the theory cannot predict the sign of this coefficient and that the interest rate was fixed. The rate of return variable was also negatively correlated with income level. Therefore, two of the explanatory variables were colinear, which could increase the variance of the estimated coefficients.

A significant interest rate term is found in the aggregate time series regression when the expenditure ratio cross section equations determine the income component of total expenditures. The estimated coefficient is negative, indicating that the substitution effect outweighs the income effect of a change in the after-tax rate of return. This result means that only aggregate level average tax-rate changes affect individual expenditures and savings through the after-tax rate of return. As a result, the role of the marginal tax rate of an individual is reduced to the implied changes in average tax rates.

From the theory discussion above, marginal rates affect the after-tax rate of return to savings and this impacts on savings and expenditures at the individual level. That the current model only includes tax rates in the aggregate is a problem and is an area for future research.

Tax Policies Considered

The flat tax considered is called a pure flat tax because all taxpayers at all income levels face the same rate. In this radical departure from the current system all deductions and exemptions are eliminated. A less radical change has been suggested by Bradley and Gephardt. In their plan, the current system would be simplified to three tax brackets with marginal rates ranging from 14 to 30 percent. The other major change is the elimination of many deductions. Remaining deductions would be valued at the 14 percent marginal rate. Both policies are discussed below.

Bradley-Gephardt Proposal

A simplified progressive structure has been suggested by Bradley and Gephardt as a replacement for the current system. The idea behind the proposal is to reduce statutory marginal rates and at the same time expand the tax base by eliminating many deductions and loopholes. The overall motivation of the proposal seems to be to reduce marginal tax rates to increase economic efficiency. At the same time, expanding the tax base by limiting deductions and loopholes could keep aggregate collections at current system levels, eliminating fiscal complications. In addition, limiting loopholes might make the system seem more equitable because all taxpayers would be paying close to their statutory rate. Under the current system, taxpayers with high incomes can pay very little tax by making use of deductions.

In 1982 Schedule Y, for married persons, had 14 brackets. The Bradley-Gephardt proposal compresses those 14 tax brackets into four brackets for single and married taxpayers. The proposed schedule is shown in table 6.1.

The Bradley-Gephardt scheme makes up for lower tax rates by increasing the tax base through elimination of most deductions, and reductions in the value of those that remain. The major deductions which are kept under the plan are (1) home mortgage interest, (2) state and local income and property taxes, and (3) social security and veterans benefits for low-income taxpayers. A major change under the plan is that deductions and exemptions would reduce taxable income for only the base tax rate (14 percent). Therefore one dollar of deductions would have the same value for all taxpayers. Under the current system, an additional dollar of deductions is valued at the taxpayer's marginal tax rate and therefore a one dollar deduction reduces a high-income taxpayer's liability more than a one dollar deduction for a low-income taxpayer.

A technical paper prepared by Senator Bradley's office (April 15, 1983)

Table 6.1.   Bradley-Gephardt Proposed Tax Rates

Bracket		Marginal Rates
Single	Married	
0 – 3,000	0 – 6,000	0.0*
3,000 – 25,000	6,000 – 40,000	14.0
25,000 – 37,500	40,000 – 65,000	26.0
37,500 and over	65,000 and over	30.0

* Standard Deduction Amount

claims that the proposed tax structure is "approximately revenue and distribution neutral with respect to tax liability." To show the neutrality, the technical paper compares examples of returns under the current system and also the Bradley-Gephardt plan for six single and ten married taxpayers with incomes ranging from $15,000 to over one million dollars. To summarize the differences in taxes due in the examples, taxpayers with typical returns — mostly salary and interest income and homeowner-related deductions — pay slightly lower taxes under the Bradley-Gephardt plan. Relative savings are greatest for those with high salary and interest incomes who use the standard deduction. These persons benefit from the lower rates without suffering from reduced deductions. Higher taxes are paid by those who, under current law, have high deductions relative to income and those who benefit from provisions such as reduced capital gains taxes and deductions for intangible oil drilling expenses.

The examples give an idea of those who will benefit under the Bradley-Gephardt proposal, and some indication of those who will pay more in taxes. The examples seem to indicate that almost all taxpayers will be better off in terms of taxes with only a few exceptions. This pattern may be correct, but the examples were worked out by supporters of the plan and therefore the sample tax returns might not be representative. Exact impacts should be considered more carefully before such a proposal is implemented.

To test the Bradley-Gephardt scheme exactly is difficult with the current model because the bill deals explicitly with deductions and exemptions. The model here, however, does not include these adjustments to income and focuses on effective tax rates. Recall that effective tax rates include the reductions in taxes actually paid due to deductions and exemptions.

To test a new tax structure exactly requires a model which includes deductions and exemptions by income level, income distributions by type of income and marital status of earner, and other detailed information. Because this study focuses on the expenditure and savings effects of income distribution, such a detailed tax model is not of primary interest.

However, the general impact of a Bradley-Gephardt-type proposal on taxes and expenditures can be tested. Specifically, the following two simulations test whether a three bracket system can approximate the distribution of effective rates which result from the current system. As an example, a three bracket tax system with brackets and rates similar to Bradley-Gephardt are considered in two simulations. First, a simplified Bradley-Gephardt tax structure is simulated over history to compare the aggregate level of taxes collected with the base tax law. The second simulation then corrects the simplified tax program to yield the same taxes as in the base case. This run shows the distributional impacts of the simplified structure on aggregate expenditures.

The purpose of these simulations is to test whether a four bracket system can result in tax collections similar to those under the current system both in the aggregate and in cross section. This test is important because a main motivation behind simplified tax structure proposals is to achieve a system with low marginal rates but which is as progressive as the current system. It is important to remember that the simulation is not a test of the Bradley-Gephardt proposal, but is a test of a simplified tax structure similar to Bradley-Gephardt.

First Bradley-Gephardt-Type Simulation

The simplified Bradley-Gephardt tax law is based on the following assumptions. First, to combine the single and married tax brackets into one set of brackets necessary for the model, the bracket boundaries are assumed to be a weighted average of the Bradley-Gephardt boundaries, where the weights are the relative number of unrelated individuals and families. In principle, this assumption could be avoided because the model contains separate distributions for unrelated individuals and families. However, this would require assuming that all families file joint returns and all individuals file single returns. This would overstate family tax rates because a family can legally reduce its effective rate by filing more than one return. Next, the brackets are indexed for inflation. Although indexation is not in the Bradley-Gephardt proposal, it is done because of the large change in prices over the historical sample. Although actual tax brackets have not been specifically indexed, there has been some implicit indexation through rate reductions (e.g., 1964) and increases in the personal exemption amount (e.g., 1979).

The resulting aggregate tax collections are compared with base values in table 6.2. The results are surprisingly close to the base values, especially in recent years. For the period 1979–1981, the Bradley-Gephardt-type plan predicts tax collections with a 2.4 percent average difference from the base case. Other years are also close, with the largest difference in the 11 percent range. To some degree, this verifies the claim in the technical paper from Senator Bradley's office that the simplified tax schedule would produce the same aggregate collections as the current system. However, because the standard deduction amount was assumed and personal exemptions were ignored, this simulation is not a good test of the claim.

Second Bradley-Gephart-Type Simulation

This simulation uses the same tax brackets as the first Bradley-Gephardt-type run but adjusts the marginal rates to reproduce the aggregate taxes in

Table 6.2.   Personal Federal Taxes — Bradley-Gephardt Simulation

Date	History	First Bradley-Gephardt Simulation	Difference	% Difference
1960	43.642	41.235	2.407	5.515
1961	44.702	42.977	1.725	3.859
1962	48.638	46.609	2.028	4.170
1963	51.485	49.323	2.161	4.198
1964	48.627	54.208	-5.581	-11.476
1965	53.949	60.053	-6.104	-11.314
1966	61.693	66.947	-5.253	-8.515
1967	67.478	72.433	-4.955	-7.343
1968	79.664	79.947	-0.283	-0.355
1969	95.109	88.712	6.397	6.726
1970	92.607	94.288	-1.681	-1.815
1971	90.309	100.064	-9.755	-10.802
1972	108.207	111.465	-3.258	-3.011
1973	144.706	127.032	-12.326	-10.746
1974	131.264	135.796	-4.532	-3.453
1975	125.833	140.663	-14.829	-11.785
1976	147.270	156.978	-9.708	-6.592
1977	170.060	178.145	-8.085	-4.754
1978	194.928	205.137	-10.208	-5.237
1979	230.565	235.024	-4.459	-1.934
1980	257.543	254.020	3.523	1.368
1981	298.059	286.703	11.357	3.810

the base. For each year, the three marginal rates are multiplied by the adjustment factor necessary to reproduce the base case collections exactly. This simulation is a test of the distributional impact of a simplified progressive tax structure.

If the claim of the Bradley technical paper is true — that the restructuring of the tax law does not change the distribution of personal taxes or the aggregate level — there should be no expenditure or savings effect in the current model. If there is no change in aggregate taxes or the distribution of liabilities, there will be no direct impact on expenditures or savings in the current model. Recall that in the cross section, changes in tax rates affect expenditures through changes in disposable income. Marginal tax rates have no direct impact on expenditures and savings because the economic linkage, the after-tax rate of return on savings, only showed significant estimation results at the aggregate level. Even at the aggregate level, the rate-of-return effect is very small compared to the impact through disposable income.

The simulation is surprising because there is almost no distributional impact. For example, in terms of disposable income in 1972, the largest relative change as a result of the new tax structure for any of the 12 income classes is a 1.3 percent increase in the $4,000 to $5,000 range. It is important to note that in the *largest* income class, over $25,000, disposable income increases by only 0.2 percent. These changes can be compared to the pure flat tax simulation where disposable income in the over $25,000 income class increases by 6.2 percent.

The small impact on the distribution of disposable income translates into almost no change in aggregate expenditures. Total expenditures change by less than 0.1 percent in each year of the sample.

These small impacts on aggregate spending are understandable because the distribution of disposable income does not change. What is surprising is that a simple four bracket system can so closely approximate a much more complicated one, whereas a single bracket flat tax produces such large effects.

No specific conclusions about the Bradley-Gephardt plan can be drawn from these simulations because the model does not explicitly include deductions, which are a large part of the Bradley-Gephardt proposal. What can be said, however, is that a simplified four bracket system with tax rates in the range of Bradley-Gephardt could result in tax collections similar to the current system both in the aggregate and in the distribution over the income range.

The Bradley-Gephardt-type tax system is not simulated in conjunction with the Wharton macro model because the small changes in aggregate expenditures would give only a slight shock to the macro model. The flat tax scenario, discussed below, shows greater changes in aggregate expenditures which are fed into the macro model.

Pure Flat Tax

This section examines the pure flat tax where all taxpayers face a single tax rate. In the following simulations, there is one personal federal tax rate for all income levels. In addition, there are assumed to be no exemptions or deductions and therefore the effective as well as statutory rates are identical for all taxpayers.

Presented first is a simulation of the income distribution and expenditure model. The simulation shows the direct effects of a flat tax with no feedback on personal income. The flat tax rate is chosen to yield the base case aggregate tax collections given no change in income. The simulation is comparable with the multiplier runs in chapter five.

Joint simulations with the Wharton Long-Term macro model are then presented. The results include the effects of changes in personal income and interest rates which result from the flat-tax-induced changes in savings and expenditures.

In the first joint simulation, the tax rate for each year is chosen to exactly reproduce aggregate personal taxes in the base case given no income change. This simulation shows the macroeconomic impacts of a flat tax when the tax rate is chosen ex ante. Because aggregate income falls due to reduced expenditures, aggregate tax collections are also lower than in the base case. Part of the increase in the level of private savings goes to the increase in government dissavings, the federal deficit.

In the second joint simulation, the flat tax rate is chosen to reproduce the base level of tax collections after aggregate income has fallen. The ex post flat tax rate is therefore slightly higher than the ex ante tax rate.

In all of the simulations, the flat tax redistributes disposable income by shifting the tax burden from high- to low-income taxpayers. Table 6.3 shows the effective tax rates for one year, 1978, and the flat tax rate (12.2 percent) which yields the same revenue given no income change. The differ-

Table 6.3.   Effective Tax Rates — 1978

Adjusted Gross Income (Thousands of Dollars)			Tax Rate (Percent)	
Above	But	Below	Marginal	Average
0		2	0.068	0.137
2		4	0.784	0.569
4		6	7.488	3.336
6		7	10.449	4.978
7		8	12.928	6.038
8		9	15.580	7.160
9		10	13.992	7.880
10		11	14.854	8.544
11		12	14.758	9.084
12		13	17.485	9.756
13		14	15.915	10.213
14		15	17.354	10.705
15		20	16.885	11.764
20		25	18.410	13.241
25		30	22.554	14.934
30		50	24.101	17.799
50		100	33.141	24.959
100		200	42.070	33.515
200		500	44.671	39.890
	Over 500		48.940	44.717

Flat tax rate = 12.2 percent

ence shows the change in effective tax rates for the cross section of income levels.

The crossover point for 1978 shown in table 6.3 is between $20,000 and $25,000. Above the crossover point, effective tax rates would be reduced under the flat tax, and at lower income levels, increased. As a result, disposable income increases above this point, and falls below it.

Static Flat Tax Simulation

The cross section results are easily interpreted. By assumption, there is no change in the distribution of before-tax income. The distribution of disposable income, however, is affected. Using 1972 as an example, disposable income in the $15,000 to $20,000 bracket is the same as in the base, indicating that the crossover point for 1972 is in this range. The crossover point for 1978 (shown in table 6.1) differs from the 1972 point due to inflation and the fact that the disposable income tables presented are in constant dollars. The change in the distribution of disposable income for 1972 is shown in table 6.4. For all consumer units above $20,000, disposable income increases due to the flat tax by $1.8 billion or 4.7 percent. Below $15,000, disposable income decreases by the same amount, $1.8 billion, which is 0.5 percent of the income of consumers below $15,000. The two changes in disposable income exactly offset each other in the aggregate because of the assumption that aggregate taxes remain the same as in the base case.

Table 6.4.   Change in the Distribution of
Disposable Income Due to Flat Tax — 1972

Income Range (Thousands of Dollars)	Change in Disposable Income (Billions of Dollars)
Under 3	-1.6
3 – 4	-1.3
4 – 5	-1.5
5 – 6	-1.6
6 – 7	-1.6
7 – 8	-1.3
8 – 10	-2.4
10 – 12	-1.9
12 – 15	-1.8
15 – 20	0
20 – 25	2.4
over 25	12.4
All income levels	0

As discussed in the Bradley-Gephardt simulations, changes in expenditures due to tax rate shifts work through changes in disposable income. Effects through the after-tax rate of return only have a slight impact when the aggregate tax rate changes. Therefore, the flat tax primarily reduces aggregate personal spending by shifting disposable income from high-spending low-income consumers to lower-spending high-income consumers. Because the tax rate in this simulation is chosen ex ante and is the same as in the base case, the aggregate after-tax rate of return is the same as in the base.

Cross section expenditure results follow from the changes in the distribution of disposable income. Results from 1972 are shown in table 6.5. At income levels below the crossover point, expenditures fall because of the decreases in disposable income, and expenditures increase at income levels above the crossover point because of lower taxes and more disposable income in this range. However, expenditure changes for the two income groups are not offsetting because individual marginal propensities to consume decline as income levels rise. Therefore, the reductions in disposable income for low-income consumers result in decreases in expenditures which are greater in absolute value than the increases in expenditures by upper-income consumers. A similar result was found in the multiplier simulations in the previous chapter.

Aggregate personal taxes and therefore disposable income do not change as a result of the flat tax by assumption. Aggregate expenditures, however, fall. As was seen in the demographic multiplier experiments, an

Table 6.5. Change in the Distribution of
Consumption Due to Flat Tax — 1972

Income Range (Thousands of Dollars)	Change in Expenditures (Billions of Dollars)
Under 3	-1.5
3 - 4	-1.2
4 - 5	-1.5
5 - 6	-1.5
6 - 7	-1.4
7 - 8	-1.3
8 - 10	-2.1
10 - 12	-1.7
12 - 15	-1.5
15 - 20	- .1
20 - 25	1.7
over 25	8.3
Aggregate	-3.8

upward shift in the distribution of disposable income causes expenditures to fall because the average propensities to consume decline as income levels rise.

Aggregate Savings and Expenditures

Aggregate consumption drops by $3.7 billion in 1972. Over the six year period, personal spending falls an average of 3.3 billion in 1972 dollars, or about 0.5 percent. Aggregate savings increases by the same level as personal expenditures fall because aggregate disposable income is fixed by assumption. Therefore, real savings is 3.3 billion higher on average than in the base case. The increase in savings is shown in table 6.6. Higher savings is one of the outcomes of a flat tax predicted by its supporters.

However, these results are static in that they do not include feedback from the rest of the economy. This is an important point because, in a complete model, an exogenous change in consumption, which is the implicit result of the flat tax, will have an effect on variables exogenous in the income distribution and expenditure model. Possible changes in income are important when studying savings because savings is the difference between disposable income and expenditures. Private interest outlays and transfers to foreigners are also subtracted from disposable income to reach private savings. These are assumed fixed.

Joint Simulations of a Flat Tax with a Macro Model

To study a full economic system, the income distribution, tax and expenditure system can be combined with a macro model by joint simulation. (Incorporating the income distribution and expenditure model into a macro model is preferable to joint simulation. An earlier version of the income distribution model was merged with a small macro model. The current version was not integrated into a full model because of computer cost

Table 6.6.   Increase in Aggregate Savings
Due to Flat Tax Only

Date	Billions of 1972 Dollars
1970	2.9
1971	2.9
1972	3.8
1973	3.6
1974	3.7
1975	3.7

considerations.) Changes in expenditures as a result of the flat tax are incorporated into the macro model as exogenous adjustments to a baseline simulation. The macro model is then resimulated to show the full macro impacts.

Adjusting expenditures in the macro model can be thought of as changes in the intercepts of the expenditure equations in the macro model rather than changes in the complete equations. The process introduces an inconsistency because the macro model is solved with its original consumption equations. Decreases in income as a result of the initial shock further decrease spending based on the macro model consumption functions rather than the equations in the income distribution and expenditure model. The final results will be inconsistent if the marginal propensities to consume are different in the two models. The first-period aggregate marginal propensity to consume in the Wharton Long-Term model is 0.3. Longer-term aggregate propensities are higher, but are difficult to determine because many categories of consumer spending are identified in the model.

An attempt to eliminate the inconsistency by determining consumption completely in the income distribution model was made. The macro model was first solved holding consumption at base levels adjusted for the initial reductions due to the flat tax. The changes in income—due to the exogenous consumption drop and the simultaneously determined changes in the other income components—were then introduced into the income distribution model to capture secondary changes in consumption due to the income changes. Consumption levels in the macro model were again adjusted and the model resolved with consumption exogenous. The process was repeated several times but was abandoned because income changes were small, indicating that convergence would take many iterations. This result is understandable because consumption adjusts to income changes only once per joint simulation. Therefore many iterations of the joint system would be necessary for convergence and the simpler method was used. The Wharton model converges in six iterations given small shocks. Because of lagged variables a dynamic simulation would require six iterations per year, or 36 joint simulations.

The joint simulations are carried out for the period 1970 through 1975. The starting point, 1970, is chosen because an historical base simulation for the Wharton Long-Term model is available beginning in that year. The base simulation is a dynamic simulation which has been adjusted to reproduce history. After the first simulation period, lagged values are taken from the simulation itself. However, because the solution does not follow history exactly, the joint simulation is carried out in terms of changes from the base solution. The Wharton model is simulated for six periods because this is enough for most lags in the model to fully adjust.

Ex Ante Flat Tax Simulation

The joint process begins with the static simulation of the income distribution and expenditure model presented above. The flat tax rate yields the base level of tax collections given no income change. The resulting changes in consumption are then introduced into the Wharton macro model as exogenous reductions in expenditures. Changes in total consumption from the income distribution model are allocated into three consumption categories: durables, nondurables, and services. The changes in total personal spending are allocated into the three categories to preserve disaggregation of consumption categories in the Wharton model.

In well-specified models of the U.S. economy, such as the Wharton Long-Term model, an autonomous drop in aggregate personal spending results in a reduced level of economic activity. A lower level of personal spending initially reduces aggregate demand which then causes a lower level of personal income. Less personal income results in additional declines in aggregate demand and income. These feedback effects—initial reductions in personal spending causing reductions in personal income and further drops in personal spending—are taken into account in the macro simulation. The simulation of the income distribution and expenditure model alone gives the initial reductions in expenditures due to the flat tax alone. The macro simulation includes the feedback effects and shows the full impact of the flat tax on expenditures and savings. In addition, the macro model shows changes in investment and other key variables.

Key Macroeconomic Variables

The macroeconomic impacts of a flat tax can be seen by comparing the flat tax simulation with a base case simulation. The overall macro outcome of the flat tax is an average drop in real GNP of $4 billion, less than 0.5 percent compared with the base case. The lower level of economic activity is initially caused by reduced consumer demand. Aggregate consumer spending first falls due to the redistribution effects of the flat tax even when aggregate disposable income is held constant. When feedback through the macro economy is taken into account, the initial aggregate spending drop causes disposable income to fall by an average of $2.2 billion. On average, personal spending drops by an additional $1.4 billion in real terms.

The impact of the flat tax on key macroeconomic variables is shown in tables 6.7 and 6.8. The drop in expenditures—the initial shock—represents the major share of the change in GNP. Over the six year sample period, real consumer spending averages $4.9 billion lower in the flat tax case. Private investment is $1.0 billion lower in the first simulation year due to the flat

Table 6.7. Selected Economic Indicators — Ex Ante Flat Tax

			1970	1971	1972	1973	1974	1975
GNP	I	GROSS NATIONAL PRODUCT (72 $)------						
		HISTORY----------------------------	1085.9	1122.7	1185.5	1254.8	1248.4	1232.1
		FLAT TAX---------------------------	1081.3	1118.6	1180.9	1252.0	1245.7	1227.0
		DIFFERENCE-------------------------	-4.5	-4.1	-4.6	-2.8	-2.8	-5.1
		% DIFFERENCE-----------------------	-.4	-.4	-.4	-.2	-.2	-.4
PDGNP	I	GROSS NAT. PROD. DEFL. (1972=100.0)						
		HISTORY----------------------------	91.5	96.0	100.0	105.7	115.0	125.7
		FLAT TAX---------------------------	91.5	96.2	100.1	105.7	114.9	125.6
		DIFFERENCE-------------------------	.1	.1	.1	.0	-.1	-.1
		% DIFFERENCE-----------------------	.1	.1	.1	.0	-.1	-.1
NEHT	I	EMPLOYMENT (MILLIONS)--------------						
		HISTORY----------------------------	78.69	79.37	82.15	85.07	86.85	85.90
		FLAT TAX---------------------------	78.55	79.17	81.89	84.81	86.60	85.57
		DIFFERENCE-------------------------	-.14	-.21	-.26	-.26	-.25	-.33
		% DIFFERENCE-----------------------	-.17	-.26	-.32	-.30	-.28	-.38
CPUBT$	I	CORPORATE PROFITS BEFORE TAXES-----						
		HISTORY----------------------------	75.2	87.2	99.9	126.1	137.4	132.4
		FLAT TAX---------------------------	74.1	86.6	99.1	125.5	136.7	130.4
		DIFFERENCE-------------------------	-1.1	-.6	-.8	-.7	-.7	-2.0
		% DIFFERENCE-----------------------	-1.4	-.6	-.8	-.5	-.5	-1.5
FRMCS	B	MOODY'S CORPORATE BOND RATE,AVG(%)-						
		HISTORY----------------------------	8.51	7.95	7.63	7.79	9.01	9.54
		FLAT TAX---------------------------	8.45	7.83	7.46	7.59	8.78	9.24
		DIFFERENCE-------------------------	-.06	-.12	-.16	-.20	-.23	-.31
FRMLCDS	B	LRG TIME DEP(NEGOT CD'S),AVG(%)----						
		HISTORY----------------------------	7.57	5.00	4.65	8.40	10.21	6.41
		FLAT TAX---------------------------	7.33	4.86	4.46	8.15	9.92	5.96
		DIFFERENCE-------------------------	-.24	-.15	-.19	-.25	-.29	-.45
NRUT	I	UNEMPLOYMENT RATE (%)--------------						
		HISTORY----------------------------	4.93	5.94	5.62	4.88	5.54	8.41
		FLAT TAX---------------------------	5.10	6.18	5.92	5.15	5.80	8.75
		DIFFERENCE-------------------------	.17	.25	.30	.28	.25	.34
YPDSAVR	B	SAVINGS RATE (%)-------------------						
		HISTORY----------------------------	8.07	8.02	6.54	8.59	8.58	8.54
		FLAT TAX---------------------------	8.37	8.31	6.94	8.96	8.96	8.87
		DIFFERENCE-------------------------	.30	.29	.40	.37	.38	.33
GVSURPF$	I	SURPLUS OR DEFICIT, FEDERAL (CUR $)						
		HISTORY----------------------------	-12.3	-21.9	-17.0	-5.6	-10.7	-69.3
		FLAT TAX---------------------------	-13.3	-22.9	-18.2	-6.6	-11.7	-70.9
		DIFFERENCE-------------------------	-1.0	-1.0	-1.2	-1.0	-.9	-1.6
		% DIFFERENCE-----------------------	8.5	4.5	7.0	17.4	8.7	2.3

Table 6.8. Components of Gross National Product

		1970	1971	1972	1973	1974	1975
	--------CONSTANT 72 DOLLARS--------						
CE I	PERSONAL CONSUMPTION EXPENDITURES--						
	HISTORY---------------------------	672.1	696.9	737.0	768.1	763.6	779.6
	FLAT TAX--------------------------	668.0	692.7	731.4	763.1	758.9	774.2
	DIFFERENCE------------------------	-4.1	-4.3	-5.6	-5.0	-4.8	-5.3
	% DIFFERENCE----------------------	-.6	-.6	-.8	-.6	-.6	-.7
IBT I	GROSS PRIVATE DOMESTIC INVESTMENT--						
	HISTORY---------------------------	158.7	174.1	195.0	217.8	196.5	155.2
	FLAT TAX--------------------------	157.8	173.9	195.4	219.5	198.0	154.8
	DIFFERENCE------------------------	-.9	-.2	.5	1.7	1.5	-.4
	% DIFFERENCE----------------------	-.6	-.1	.2	.8	.8	-.3
IBF I	FIXED INVESTMENT------------------						
	HISTORY---------------------------	154.9	166.0	184.8	200.5	184.6	161.9
	FLAT TAX--------------------------	154.5	166.1	185.5	202.2	186.0	161.7
	DIFFERENCE------------------------	-.4	.1	.7	1.7	1.4	-.2
	% DIFFERENCE----------------------	-.3	.1	.4	.8	.7	-.1
IBFN I	NONRESIDENTIAL-----------------						
	HISTORY---------------------------	113.9	112.3	121.0	138.2	136.1	119.6
	FLAT TAX--------------------------	113.5	112.0	120.8	138.3	136.3	119.8
	DIFFERENCE------------------------	-.4	-.3	-.2	.2	.2	.2
	% DIFFERENCE----------------------	-.3	-.2	-.2	.1	.2	.1
IBFR I	RESIDENTIAL STRUCTURES----------						
	HISTORY---------------------------	41.0	53.7	63.8	62.4	48.6	42.3
	FLAT TAX--------------------------	41.0	54.1	64.7	63.9	49.7	41.9
	DIFFERENCE------------------------	.0	.4	.9	1.5	1.2	-.4
	% DIFFERENCE----------------------	.0	.7	1.4	2.4	2.4	-.9
IBIT I	CHANGE IN BUSINESS INVENTORIES----						
	HISTORY---------------------------	3.8	8.1	10.2	17.3	11.8	-6.7
	FLAT TAX--------------------------	3.3	7.8	9.9	17.3	12.0	-6.9
	DIFFERENCE------------------------	-.5	-.3	-.2	.0	.2	-.2
TBB I	NET EXPORTS OF GOODS AND SERVICES--						
	HISTORY---------------------------	4.0	1.5	.4	15.5	28.1	32.1
	FLAT TAX--------------------------	4.5	1.9	.9	15.9	28.6	32.7
	DIFFERENCE------------------------	.5	.4	.5	.4	.5	.6
TEB I	EXPORTS---------------------------						
	HISTORY---------------------------	70.5	70.9	77.4	97.3	108.5	103.6
	FLAT TAX--------------------------	70.5	70.8	77.3	97.2	108.5	103.6
	DIFFERENCE------------------------	.0	-.1	-.1	-.1	.0	.0
TMB I	IMPORTS---------------------------						
	HISTORY---------------------------	66.4	69.4	77.0	81.8	80.4	71.5
	FLAT TAX--------------------------	65.9	69.0	76.4	81.3	79.9	70.9
	DIFFERENCE------------------------	-.5	-.5	-.6	-.5	-.5	-.6

tax and contributes to the lower level of the GNP. By the third year of the simulation, however, lower interest rates push investment above base case levels. (Investment is discussed in detail below.) Net exports are an average of $0.5 billion higher in the flat tax simulation, somewhat offsetting the drop in GNP. The trade balance is improved because of lower levels of imports caused by reduced domestic economic activity. Government purchases of goods and services are fixed in real terms by assumption.

Prices change very little as a result of the flat tax. For example, the GNP price deflator increases by 0.1 percent in the first year of the simulation. In the short run, lower economic activity causes productivity to decline and prices to increase in the Wharton model. By the end of the simulation period, the GNP price deflator is 0.1 percent lower due to the lower level of economic activity. The lower activity level is the main factor contributing to an increase in productivity which causes prices to fall slightly.

Long-term interest rates decline by up to 0.3 percentage points. The major reason for the decline is that the money supply was assumed to be unchanged from the base case. In the Wharton model a fixed money supply and a lower level of nominal income result in lower interest rates. Lower inflation in the later years of the simulation also contribute slightly to the lower interest rates.

The fixed money supply assumption was made to produce lower interest rates and stimulate investment. The fixed money supply assumption is conservative in the sense that the macro results show a smaller increase in investment than might be expected by supporters of a flat tax.

Savings and Investment

In the macro simulation, personal expenditures are lower and savings higher due to the flat tax. For example, in 1972, real expenditures are $5.6 billion lower than in the base case. The savings rate increases by 0.5 percentage points to 6.9 percent, and personal savings is $3.1 billion higher.

The increase in savings in the macro model simulation of the flat tax is smaller than in the static simulation of the income distribution and expenditure model. In the static case personal income is held constant while in the macro simulation personal income declines, offsetting gains in savings.

One of the major goals of a flat tax cited by its proponents is a higher level of investment. Flat tax supporters suggest that an increase in savings will result in an increase in investment which will lead to a greater and more productive capital stock. However, an increase in private savings need not result in an increase in investment in the capital stock. National income accounting identities require that changes in gross savings equal changes in gross investment. While the flat tax simulation shows a higher level of personal savings, investment in the capital stock — business fixed investment — actually declines in the first three years of the simulation. To understand this pattern, the components of gross investment and the sources of gross savings are discussed below.

The major components of gross investment are net foreign and private domestic investment. The flat tax causes net foreign investment to decline because of improvements in trade balances. Lower levels of domestic activity reduce import needs and the net exports balance improves. By identity, net foreign investment declines.

The largest component of private domestic investment is business fixed investment and it is this investment component which adds to the productive capital stock. The flat tax simulation shows slightly lower levels of business fixed investment in the first three years of the experiment. The last three years show higher levels than in the base case, but over the six year period, cumulative real business fixed investment is $0.3 billion lower. Therefore the capital stock is actually reduced as a result of the flat tax.

Business fixed investment initially falls compared to the base case because of the lower levels of economic activity. While stimulating aggregate private savings, the flat tax reduces personal spending and therefore aggregate demand. Investment falls — compared with the base — because a smaller capital stock is required to meet the lower levels of aggregate demand.

Business fixed investment increases in the fourth through sixth years of the simulation — again compared with the base case. By the fourth year, lower interest rates offset the impact of lower activity and business fixed investment is higher than in the base example. However, as noted above, cumulative investment is lower over the six year period.

Residential investment in the flat tax simulation, however, exceeds the base case levels in all but one year. Real residential investment increases because of the reductions in interest rates. The interest rate effects, however, are damped slightly by the lower levels of personal income.

Compared with business fixed investment, residential investment is more sensitive to interest rates and less sensitive to economic activity. Therefore, most of the gains in domestic investment due to the flat-tax-induced lower interest rates occur in the residential sector.

The last component of domestic investment — changes in business inventories — are not greatly affected by the flat tax. Inventory swings follow the business cycle, which is not changed very much in the flat tax simulation.

The changes in gross investment resulting from the flat tax are smaller than the changes in private savings. For example, in 1972, private savings in the flat tax simulation is $3.1 billion higher than in the base case. However, gross investment is only $1.0 billion more. The discrepancy can be accounted for in other uses of savings—primarily government deficits which are discussed below.

Uses of Savings

Higher levels of private savings do not necessarily translate directly into more investment. National income accounting identities require that gross savings always equals gross investment. The major components of gross savings are private savings, retained earnings, capital consumption allowances, and the total government surplus. Gross investment includes fixed investment, inventory changes, and net foreign investment. In any simulation, a change in any one of these categories must be balanced by a change in another category. Therefore, it is not necessarily true that a change in personal savings implies an equal change in investment.

In this simulation, the increase in the level of savings is partially offset by higher government deficits and reduced levels of retained earnings. The government deficit increases because of lower tax collections, including personal, indirect business, and corporate taxes. Retained earnings fall because corporate earnings decline more than dividend payments. On the other hand, foreign investment increases because the trade balance becomes more positive. This shift adds to investment potential. Changes in the sources and uses of savings are shown in Table 6.9.

Ex Post Flat Tax Simulation

In the previous simulation, aggregate taxes fell because the flat tax rate was chosen to yield the base level of tax collections at the base income. The drop in income caused aggregate personal taxes to fall and lower taxes contributed to a higher federal deficit. Higher deficits are a problem in the current political environment and, if a flat tax were to be imposed, it is likely that the tax rate would be chosen to yield the base level of taxes after personal income has adjusted. In addition, in an accounting framework with all other variables held constant, higher deficits reduce investment by lowering total domestic savings. However, this is not a causal relationship and maintaining a given level of taxes will not necessarily increase investment. A higher flat tax rate is likely to reduce consumer expenditures more, resulting in a lower level of GNP. Key economic indicators and components of GNP are shown in tables 6.10 and 6.11.

This simulation tests the flat tax when the flat rate is chosen to yield the base level of personal taxes after income has adjusted. The simulation process is the same as in the previous example. First, the flat tax with the ex

Table 6.9.   Sources and Uses of Gross Saving

			1970	1971	1972	1973	1974	1975
SVG$		GROSS SAVING-----------------------						
		HISTORY-----------------------------	149.2	162.1	186.7	235.7	229.4	218.5
		FLAT TAX----------------------------	148.9	162.5	187.9	237.9	231.9	218.8
		DIFFERENCE--------------------------	-.2	.4	1.2	2.2	2.4	.3
SVGP$		GROSS PRIVATE SAVING---------------						
		HISTORY-----------------------------	159.5	181.4	190.2	227.9	232.9	282.3
		FLAT TAX----------------------------	160.7	183.2	193.1	231.2	236.4	284.6
		DIFFERENCE--------------------------	1.2	1.8	2.8	3.4	3.5	2.4
YPDSAV$	I	PERSONAL SAVING--------------------						
		HISTORY-----------------------------	56.1	60.3	53.0	78.6	85.6	93.6
		FLAT TAX----------------------------	58.1	62.4	56.2	81.7	89.2	96.8
		DIFFERENCE--------------------------	2.0	2.1	3.1	3.2	3.6	3.2
RET$	I	UNDISTRIBUTED CORPORATE PROFITS--						
		HISTORY-----------------------------	18.5	26.7	33.9	50.0	55.5	51.1
		FLAT TAX----------------------------	17.9	26.4	33.5	49.7	55.2	50.0
		DIFFERENCE--------------------------	-.6	-.3	-.5	-.4	-.4	-1.1
IVAC$	B	CORPORATE INVENTORY VALUATION ADJ						
		HISTORY-----------------------------	-6.6	-4.6	-6.5	-19.9	-39.7	-11.7
		FLAT TAX----------------------------	-6.8	-4.7	-6.5	-19.3	-39.5	-11.5
		DIFFERENCE--------------------------	-.2	-.1	.1	.6	.2	.3
		% DIFFERENCE----------------------	3.4	1.9	-1.3	-2.8	-.6	-2.1
CCAT$	I	CAPITAL CONSUMPTION ALLOWANCES---						
		HISTORY-----------------------------	88.1	96.5	106.4	116.5	135.9	159.4
		FLAT TAX----------------------------	88.1	96.6	106.5	116.5	135.9	159.4
		DIFFERENCE--------------------------	.1	.1	.1	.0	.0	.0
		% DIFFERENCE----------------------	.1	.1	.1	.0	.0	.0
GVSURPF$	I	FEDERAL----------------------------						
		HISTORY-----------------------------	-12.3	-21.9	-17.0	-5.6	-10.7	-69.3
		FLAT TAX----------------------------	-13.3	-22.9	-18.2	-6.6	-11.7	-70.9
		DIFFERENCE--------------------------	-1.0	-1.0	-1.2	-1.0	-.9	-1.6
IBG$		GROSS INVESTMENT-------------------						
		HISTORY-----------------------------	147.7	166.0	189.7	236.6	233.7	224.0
		FLAT TAX----------------------------	147.4	166.4	190.9	238.7	236.1	224.3
		DIFFERENCE--------------------------	-.2	.4	1.2	2.2	2.4	.3
IBT$	I	GROSS PRIVATE DOMESTIC INVESTMENT						
		HISTORY-----------------------------	144.3	166.7	195.0	230.0	229.4	206.5
		FLAT TAX----------------------------	143.6	166.7	195.6	231.7	231.0	205.7
		DIFFERENCE--------------------------	-.7	.0	.6	1.7	1.5	-.7
TBBNFI$	I	NET FOREIGN INVESTMENT-----------						
		HISTORY-----------------------------	3.3	-.7	-5.3	6.6	4.2	17.5
		FLAT TAX----------------------------	3.8	-.3	-4.7	7.0	5.1	18.5
		DIFFERENCE--------------------------	.5	.4	.6	.5	.9	1.0

Table 6.10 Selected Economic Indicators—Ex Post Flat Tax

			1970	1971	1972	1973	1974	1975
GNP	I	GROSS NATIONAL PRODUCT (72 $)------						
		HISTORY-----------------------------	1085.9	1122.7	1185.5	1254.8	1248.4	1232.1
		FLAT TAX, EX POST RATE-------------	1081.0	1118.4	1180.7	1251.6	1245.4	1226.3
		DIFFERENCE-------------------------	-4.9	-4.3	-4.8	-3.2	-3.0	-5.8
		% DIFFERENCE-----------------------	-.4	-.4	-.4	-.3	-.2	-.5
PDGNP	I	GROSS NAT. PROD. DEFL. (1972=100.0)						
		HISTORY-----------------------------	91.5	96.0	100.0	105.7	115.0	125.7
		FLAT TAX, EX POST RATE-------------	91.5	96.2	100.1	105.7	114.9	125.6
		DIFFERENCE-------------------------	.1	.1	.1	.0	-.1	-.1
		% DIFFERENCE-----------------------	.1	.1	.1	.0	-.1	-.1
NEHT	I	EMPLOYMENT (MILLIONS)--------------						
		HISTORY-----------------------------	78.69	79.37	82.15	85.07	86.85	85.90
		FLAT TAX, EX POST RATE-------------	78.54	79.16	81.87	84.79	86.58	85.54
		DIFFERENCE-------------------------	-.15	-.22	-.27	-.28	-.27	-.36
		% DIFFERENCE-----------------------	-.18	-.28	-.33	-.33	-.31	-.42
CPUBT$	I	CORPORATE PROFITS BEFORE TAXES-----						
		HISTORY-----------------------------	75.2	87.2	99.9	126.1	137.4	132.4
		FLAT TAX, EX POST RATE-------------	74.0	86.6	99.1	125.3	136.7	130.2
		DIFFERENCE-------------------------	-1.2	-.6	-.8	-.8	-.7	-2.2
		% DIFFERENCE-----------------------	-1.5	-.7	-.8	-.6	-.5	-1.7
FRMCS	B	MOODY'S CORPORATE BOND RATE,AVG(%)-						
		HISTORY-----------------------------	8.51	7.95	7.63	7.79	9.01	9.54
		FLAT TAX, EX POST RATE-------------	8.44	7.82	7.45	7.57	8.76	9.21
		DIFFERENCE-------------------------	-.07	-.13	-.17	-.22	-.25	-.34
FRMLCDS	B	LRG TIME DEP(NEGOT CD'S),AVG(%)----						
		HISTORY-----------------------------	7.57	5.00	4.65	8.40	10.21	6.41
		FLAT TAX, EX POST RATE-------------	7.31	4.85	4.45	8.12	9.90	5.91
		DIFFERENCE-------------------------	-.26	-.15	-.21	-.28	-.31	-.50
NRUT	I	UNEMPLOYMENT RATE (%)--------------						
		HISTORY-----------------------------	4.93	5.94	5.62	4.88	5.54	8.41
		FLAT TAX, EX POST RATE-------------	5.12	6.20	5.93	5.17	5.82	8.78
		DIFFERENCE-------------------------	.18	.26	.31	.30	.27	.37
YPDSAVR	B	SAVINGS RATE (%)-------------------						
		HISTORY-----------------------------	8.07	8.02	6.54	8.59	8.58	8.54
		FLAT TAX, EX POST RATE-------------	8.37	8.31	6.94	8.97	8.95	8.87
		DIFFERENCE-------------------------	.30	.30	.40	.37	.38	.33
GVSURPF$	I	SURPLUS OR DEFICIT, FEDERAL (CUR $)						
		HISTORY-----------------------------	-12.3	-21.9	-17.0	-5.6	-10.7	-69.3
		FLAT TAX, EX POST RATE-------------	-13.2	-22.8	-18.0	-6.4	-11.4	-70.7
		DIFFERENCE-------------------------	-1.0	-.9	-1.1	-.8	-.6	-1.4
		% DIFFERENCE-----------------------	8.0	4.2	6.3	14.4	5.9	2.0

Table 6.11 Selected Components of Gross National Product

			1970	1971	1972	1973	1974	1975
		--------CONSTANT 72 DOLLARS--------						
CE	I	PERSONAL CONSUMPTION EXPENDITURES--						
		HISTORY----------------------------	672.1	696.9	737.0	768.1	763.6	779.6
		FLAT TAX, EX POST RATE-------------	667.8	692.5	731.2	762.6	758.5	773.6
		DIFFERENCE-------------------------	-4.4	-4.5	-5.9	-5.5	-5.2	-6.0
		% DIFFERENCE-----------------------	-.7	-.6	-.8	-.7	-.7	-.8
IBT	I	GROSS PRIVATE DOMESTIC INVESTMENT--						
		HISTORY----------------------------	158.7	174.1	195.0	217.8	196.5	155.2
		FLAT TAX, EX POST RATE-------------	157.7	173.9	195.5	219.6	198.1	154.7
		DIFFERENCE-------------------------	-1.0	-.2	.5	1.8	1.7	-.5
		% DIFFERENCE-----------------------	-.6	-.1	.3	.8	.9	-.3
IBF	I	FIXED INVESTMENT------------------						
		HISTORY----------------------------	154.9	166.0	184.8	200.5	184.6	161.9
		FLAT TAX, EX POST RATE-------------	154.4	166.1	185.5	202.3	186.1	161.7
		DIFFERENCE-------------------------	-.4	.2	.7	1.8	1.5	-.3
		% DIFFERENCE-----------------------	-.3	.1	.4	.9	.8	-.2
IBFN	I	NONRESIDENTIAL------------------						
		HISTORY----------------------------	113.9	112.3	121.0	138.2	136.1	119.6
		FLAT TAX, EX POST RATE-------------	113.5	112.0	120.8	138.3	136.3	119.8
		DIFFERENCE-------------------------	-.4	-.3	-.2	.2	.2	.1
		% DIFFERENCE-----------------------	-.4	-.2	-.2	.1	.2	.1
IBFR	I	RESIDENTIAL STRUCTURES----------						
		HISTORY----------------------------	41.0	53.7	63.8	62.4	48.6	42.3
		FLAT TAX, EX POST RATE-------------	41.0	54.1	64.7	64.0	49.8	41.9
		DIFFERENCE-------------------------	.0	.4	1.0	1.6	1.3	-.4
		% DIFFERENCE-----------------------	.0	.8	1.5	2.6	2.6	-1.0
IBIT	I	CHANGE IN BUSINESS INVENTORIES----						
		HISTORY----------------------------	3.8	8.1	10.2	17.3	11.8	-6.7
		FLAT TAX, EX POST RATE-------------	3.3	7.7	9.9	17.3	12.0	-7.0
		DIFFERENCE-------------------------	-.6	-.4	-.2	.0	.2	-.2
TBB	I	NET EXPORTS OF GOODS AND SERVICES--						
		HISTORY----------------------------	4.0	1.5	.4	15.5	28.1	32.1
		FLAT TAX, EX POST RATE-------------	4.6	1.9	1.0	16.0	28.6	32.8
		DIFFERENCE-------------------------	.5	.4	.5	.5	.5	.6
		% DIFFERENCE-----------------------	12.8	27.5	123.9	3.1	1.9	2.0
TEB	I	EXPORTS---------------------------						
		HISTORY----------------------------	70.5	70.9	77.4	97.3	108.5	103.6
		FLAT TAX, EX POST RATE-------------	70.5	70.8	77.3	97.2	108.5	103.6
		DIFFERENCE-------------------------	.0	-.1	-.1	-.1	.0	.0
TMB	I	IMPORTS---------------------------						
		HISTORY----------------------------	66.4	69.4	77.0	81.8	80.4	71.5
		FLAT TAX, EX POST RATE-------------	65.9	68.9	76.4	81.2	79.9	70.8
		DIFFERENCE-------------------------	-.6	-.5	-.6	-.6	-.6	-.6

post tax rate is simulated in the income distribution and expenditure model. Changes in consumption are then fed into the macro model.

The ex post tax rate is only slightly higher — about 0.3 percent — than the ex ante rate. For example, in 1972, the flat tax rate increases from 12.28 to 12.32, 0.04 percentage points. Because the increase is so small, the simulation is very similar to the previous run.

Macroeconomic Results

The ex post flat tax causes savings to increase and economic activity to fall compared to the base case. For example, in 1972, private savings is $2.1 billion higher due to a $5.9 billion drop in consumer spending which is offset by a $1.8 billion decrease in disposable income. Real GNP is $4.6 billion lower.

Total real investment is lower than in the base case in the first two years of the simulation and is higher in the next three. Changes in residential investment dominate changes in total investment because the housing sector is more interest sensitive. Business investment declines in the first three years of the simulation because of lower economic activity. Over the six year period, the sum of real business fixed investment is $0.3 billion lower despite higher investment levels in the last three years.

Comparison to Ex Ante Simulation

As mentioned above, the ex post tax rate is only slightly higher — about 0.04 percentage points — than the ex ante tax rate. As a result, the two simulations are very similar. However there are some differences. GNP is lower in the ex post case by less than 0.1 percent. Real consumption is also lower by the same order of magnitude.

Personal federal taxes are higher in the ex post run by assumption. As a result, the federal deficit is $1.2 billion lower over the six year period in the ex post run.

Gross savings, which includes private savings and the government surplus, however, is only slightly different in the ex post case. The lower deficits are offset by lower savings due to the lower level of economic activity. Retained earnings, another component of gross savings, is also lower in the ex post case. As a result, gross savings is only $0.4 billion higher over the entire sample period in the ex post simulation compared with the ex ante run.

Differences in gross investment exactly match the differences in gross savings. However, the difference in business fixed investment is minimal and most of the change in gross investment is in the residential investment and foreign investment categories.

Total government revenues are lower in this simulation compared with the base because of lower collections from corporations and indirect business taxes. Simulations holding government revenues at base levels are possible. Corporate profit taxes could be increased, but this might reduce investment. Indirect business taxes could be raised, but this measure would be reflected in prices. Which method or combination of methods chosen is difficult to predict because lower prices and higher investment are both goals of the flat tax.

Summary and Conclusion

The Bradley-Gephardt proposal is first considered. In this proposal, the tax system is reduced to three brackets with marginal rates ranging from 14 to 30 percent. At the same time many deductions are eliminated and those that remain only reduce income taxes at the base 14 percent rate.

Because the income distribution and expenditure model does not include deductions and exemptions specifically, the Bradley-Gephardt proposal cannot be simulated exactly. However, a simplified version of the bill is tested to see if a three-bracket tax system with rates similar to Bradley-Gephardt could replace the current system with little impact on the distribution of disposable income. The results indicate that the distribution of taxes under the current system can be closely reproduced using a simplified system. Thus the structure of personal federal tax rates could be simplified without major changes to the distribution of disposable income.

Some warnings should be given. First, the model does not include many of the beneficial effects claimed by the proponents of reduced marginal rates. First on the list is an increased incentive to work. The labor supply issue is complicated because of offsetting income and substitution effects of a change in after-tax wages and aggregation problems similar to the savings problem.

The flat tax simulations presented in this chapter indicate that a restructuring of personal tax rates can lead to changes in consumer spending and savings both in the aggregate and in the cross section. When only considering distributional issues (assuming equal aggregate taxes) the pure flat tax simulation shows that real personal expenditures could drop by 0.5 percent as a direct result of the tax law change. This implies an increase in aggregate savings of $10.3 billion in 1981.

The full income feedback simulations indicate a smaller increase in savings than the simulations of the expenditure model alone. The flat tax causes a reduction in aggregate personal spending by redistributing disposable income from low- to high-income consumers. However, reduced aggregate expenditures cause income to fall. Savings do go up because of lower personal spending, but the gain in savings is reduced due to lower income.

In the ex ante simulation where personal taxes are lower than in the base case, private savings increases by an average of $3.1 billion. The personal savings rate increases by 0.2 percentage points. Gains in investment are smaller than the increases in savings. The higher savings rate comes at the expense of lower economic activity and therefore the need for capital declines. In addition, higher government deficits and reduced retained earnings account for some of the increase in personal savings.

The sum of real business fixed investment for the six-year simulation period is lower in the flat tax simulation. Lower levels of economic activity reduce the need for capital, and investment is lower in the early years of the experiment. Business investment is above the base case in later years due to lower interest rates.

A second flat tax simulation in which the tax rate is chosen to reproduce the same levels of aggregate tax collections as in the base case is also presented. In the second simulation, additional dissavings by the federal government due to lower personal tax collections are reduced by assuming a higher tax rate. However, some of the higher level of personal savings still is offset by a greater government deficit. Lower levels of economic activity reduce corporate and indirect business taxes and cause higher levels of spending on transfer payments. An even higher level of tax rates could be used to maintain a given level of government dissavings, but this is left for future research.

One purpose of the flat tax is to stimulate investment by increasing personal savings. The flat tax results in higher levels of savings, but income falls and the need for capital and investment declines. Lower interest rates stimulate investment in the later years of the simulation, but by less than the initial declines, and the final capital stock is smaller due to the flat tax.

Other considerations include the potential revaluation of assets because changes in the tax laws will alter their after-tax rate of return. Two obvious examples are the value of owner-occupied housing and tax exempt government bonds. In the case of housing, if the home mortgage deduction is eliminated, the value of the housing stock will drop because the effective price of owner-occupied housing will increase. If the price of a given house is determined by the stream of future rents, then a decrease in the effective rental price will result in a drop in the value. This might be offset by increases in disposable income because consumers will have more disposable income to spend on housing, which would bid up the rental prices.

Summaries and Conclusion

Alternative Personal Federal Tax Rate Structures

In the past few years, much attention has been focused on personal tax rates. In 1981, the Economic Recovery and Tax Act reduced all personal tax rates by 23 percent over a three-year period. A maximum rate of 50 percent was also imposed. Tax cut proponents suggest that, by reducing marginal tax rates, consumers will save more, and more savings will lead to more investment and productivity.

In addition to the 1981 tax cuts, there have been proposals to restructure the current system by reducing high tax rates and making up for the lost revenues by limiting the tax value of deductions and exemptions. At the extreme is a pure flat tax where all tax payers face the same rate. More like the current system is the Bradley-Gephardt proposal, which has three slightly progressive tax brackets with a maximum marginal rate of 30 percent. Deductions and exemptions under the proposal would be scaled back and those remaining, such as the home ownership deductions, would only be valued at the lowest tax rate.

Theory

Economic theory does not give a clear-cut prediction of the impact of a change in tax rates on aggregate consumption. At the individual level, the theory predicts two offsetting impacts. For a reduction in tax rates, a consumer will substitute consumption for savings because of the increased incentive to save. On the other hand, the consumer will have more disposable income and he can consume more now while still maintaining at least as high a level of future consumption. Thus, a tax cut might cause an increase or decrease in an individual's expenditures depending on the relative strengths of the substitution and income effects.

The second theoretical problem in analyzing a restructured tax schedule is that, even if the reaction of individual consumers were known, consumers at different income levels would be affected in different ways. A flat tax would reduce tax rates for some and increase rates for others. Therefore, to know the aggregate result, consumers at all income levels need to be studied, and their reactions added up.

To study aggregate results through individual consumer responses requires a new approach to aggregation. Rather than looking at an aggregate consumption function, this study develops a model which accounts for consumer behavior at the micro level. In doing so, consistent aggregation — the summing over individuals without losing information — is in theory assured.

Model Structure

The new tax and expenditure model arrives at aggregate consumption by adding up the expenditures of consumer units at all levels of income. Before expenditures are calculated, taxes at these income levels are computed. Therefore, tax rates by income level are explicitly included and changes to tax structures are easily studied. Any change in tax rate by income level including a pure flat tax can be simulated.

To build the new tax and expenditure system, cross section and time series information are combined. From cross section data, tax rates by income level are calculated. Cross section expenditure equations are estimated using two different approaches. First, the ratios of total expenditures to disposable income are calculated for each income interval reported in the 1972 Consumer Expenditure survey. For all years of the historical sample, expenditures for a consumer unit are basically calculated as the product of the consumer unit's disposable income and the appropriate expenditure ratio. The second approach makes use of three semilog Engel curves estimated from the same data. Expenditures in the three goods categories are calculated for consumer units by evaluating these equations at all income levels over history. However, poor simulation results caused the demand equation approach to be abandoned.

To aggregate the cross section taxes and expenditures, a gamma income distribution is used to determine the number of consumers at each income level. Two income distributions, one for families and one for unrelated individuals, are estimated for each year of the historical period. The income distributions combine the cross section taxes and expenditures into time series. Price and interest rate effects are included at this point.

Although this idea of combining cross section and time series information with an income distribution is not widely used, it is not new. Klein (1962) first proposed determining aggregate expenditures by combining one cross section budget study with yearly income distributions. Tobin and

Dolde (1971) implemented the general scheme to study monetary linkages to consumption but essentially made up the coefficients of the cross section micro equations. Their focus was the method of simulating a micro equation rather than specific results. More recently, Jorgenson, Lau and Stoker included distributional information in an aggregate consumption function. However, they focused more on the allocation of spending over goods rather than on the consumption-savings decision.

This study is unique in that it focuses on the impact of a restructured tax system using the distribution of income. Other studies, such as Boskin (1978) and Howry and Hymans (1978) have examined the effects of tax rates on consumption and savings, but because these studies use the aggregate average tax rate they cannot be used to test alternative tax rate structures. To do this it is necessary to include the income distribution.

Empirical Results

Using the newly developed model shows that a flat tax will cause savings to increase. Under a flat tax which generates the same revenue as the current system, the tax burden is shifted from the high- to the low- and middle-income levels. Aggregate expenditures fall and savings increase because high-income consumers spend proportionally less and save proportionally more of their disposable income than do lower-income consumers. Therefore shifting disposable income to higher-income consumer units will reduce expenditures and increase savings at the aggregate level.

In a static simulation where aggregate income is fixed, savings increases due to the expenditure drop only. However, aggregate income will fall as a result of the flat-tax-induced shift in savings and spending. To study the full economic effects, the income distribution and expenditure model is simulated in conjunction with the Wharton Long-Term model. Lower aggregate income caused by lower levels of spending cause further spending reductions. The final result shows that the flat tax causes aggregate income, taxes, and expenditures to fall, and savings to increase. Over the period 1970 through 1975, the flat tax simulation results in 2.5 percent more savings than the base case. However, business-fixed investment — expected to increase by flat tax supporters — actually falls. Lower levels of economic activity resulting from reduced personal consumption require a smaller capital stock for production. Business-fixed investment falls. Lower interest rates, however, cause residential investment to go up.

Conclusion

Despite some shortcomings, the model does allow the savings and expenditure impacts of alternative personal tax structures to be studied. By including the distribution of income in the calculation of taxes and expenditures, the impacts of tax policies which affect specific income levels can be simulated. Joint simulation with the Wharton Long-Term model allows the impacts of initial savings and expenditure shifts on the macro economy to be studied.

Personal federal taxes are the joint result of the estimated income distribution and the effective tax rates. Without adjustments, aggregate taxes are predicted over history with an average error of 5 percent. This is a good result considering that taxes are constructed using the income distribution and effective rates which come from different data sources.

Expenditures are predicted in two ways and the methods can be distinguished by the cross section expenditure equations. The expenditure ratio method computes spending at each income level based on the ratio of expenditures to disposable income in the 1972 Consumer Expenditure survey. The demand equation approach utilizes three semilog demand equations estimated from the same data.

Using the expenditure ratio approach, aggregate predicted expenditures fit historical data closely and acceptable multiplier properties are observed.

Using the demand equation approach, aggregate total expenditures are also predicted closely. However, the calculated income response properties are unacceptable and the demand equation approach is abandoned. Further research using alternative specifications and data sources might produce more reasonable results.

The simulation results indicate that a flat personal tax will result in higher aggregate savings and a higher savings rate. In the flat tax simulations, the level of savings increases by an average of 4.0 percent and the savings rate increases by 0.3 percentage points. However, in the macro simulations higher levels of personal savings do not result in more business investment. Lower interest rates stimulate residential investment relatively more. Lower levels of economic activity reduce the need for capital, and business fixed investment declines. Therefore, implementation of a flat tax will not lead to the desired goals of more business investment and a greater capital stock.

Bibliography

Aitchison, John and James Brown. (1957). *The Lognormal Distribution*. Cambridge: Cambridge University Press.

Ando, Albert and Franco Modigliani. (1963). "The Life Cycle Hypothesis of Savings: Aggregate Implications and Tests," *American Economic Review*, Vol. 53, May, pp. 55–84.

Behravesh, Nariman. (1980). "Supply Side Economics, An Analysis of the Prototype Wedge Model." Unpublished report, Washington, D.C.: The Congressional Budget Office.

Boskin, Michael J. (1978). "Taxation, Savings, and the Rate of Interest," *Journal of Political Economy*, Vol. 86, April, pp. S3–S27.

Bradley, William. (1983, April 15). Press Release.

Branson, William. (1972). *Macroeconomic Theory and Policy*. New York: Harper and Row.

Champernowne, David. (1953). "A Model of Income Distribution," *Economic Journal*, Vol. 63, June, pp. 318–351.

Cramer, J. S. (1969). *Empirical Econometrics*. New York: John Wiley & Sons, Inc.

Durbin, J. (1953). "A Note on Regression when there is Extraneous Information About One of the Coefficients," *Journal of the American Statistical Association*, December, pp. 799–808.

Farrell, M. J. (1953–54). "Some Aggregation Problems in Demand Analysis," *Review of Economic Studies*, Vol. 21, pp. 193–203.

Friedman, Milton. (1957). *A Theory of the Consumption Function*. Princeton: Princeton University Press.

Green, H. A. John. (1964). *Aggregation in Economic Analysis*. Princeton: Princeton University Press.

Hall, Robert. (1978). "Stochastic Implications of the Life Cycle-Permanent Income Hypothesis: Theory and Evidence," *Journal of Political Economy*, Vol. 86, no. 6, pp. 971–989.

Howrey, E. Philip and Saul H. Hymans. (1978). "The Measurement and Determination of Loanable-funds Savings," *Brookings Papers on Economic Activity, Vol. 3*, pp. 655–685.

Itzkovich, Zvi. (1978). *Estimation of a Dynamic Expenditure System Using Cross Section and Time-Series Data*. Unpublished Ph.D. Dissertation. Philadelphia, Pa: University of Pennsylvania.

Johnston, J. (1972). *Econometric Methods*, second edition. New York: McGraw-Hill.

Jorgensen, Dale W., Lawrence J. Lau and Thomas M. Stoker. (1981). "The Transcendental Logarithmic Model of Aggregate Consumer Behavior." Unpublished manuscript.

Klein, Lawrence R. (1962). *An Introduction to Econometrics*. Englewood Cliffs, N.J.: Prentice-Hall.

Kuznets, Simon. (1946). *National Product Since 1869*. New York: National Bureau of Economic Research.

McDonald, James B. and Michael R. Ransom. (1979). "Functional Forms, Estimation Techniques and the Distribution of Income," *Econometrica*, Vol. 47, November, pp. 1513–1525.

Mood, Alexander, Franklin Graybill, and Duane Boes. (1974). *Introduction to the Theory of Statistics*. New York: McGraw-Hill.

Musgrave, Richard A. and Peggy B. Musgrave. (1976). *Public Finance in Theory and Practice*. New York: McGraw-Hill.

Pechman, Joseph A. (1977). *Federal Tax Policy*, third edition. Washington, D.C.: The Brookings Institution.

Petersen, Hans-Georg. (1979). "Effects of Growing Incomes on Classified Income Distributions, the Derived Lorenz Curve, and Gini Indices," *Econometrica*, Vol. 47, no. 1, pp. 183–198.

Phlips, Louis. (1974). *Applied Consumption Analysis*. Amsterdam: North-Holland Publishing Co.

Prais, S. J. and H. S. Houthaker. (1955). *The Analysis of Family Budgets*. Cambridge: Cambridge University Press.

Sahota, Gian Singh. (1978). "Theories of Personal Income Distribution: A Survey," *Journal of Economic Literature*, Vol. 16, March, pp. 1–55.

Salem, A. B. Z. and T. D. Mount. (1974). "A Convenient Descriptive Model of Income Distribution: The Gamma Density," *Econometrica*, Vol. 42, no. 6, November, pp. 1115–1127.

Singh, S. K. and G. S. Maddala. (1976). "A Function for Size Distribution of Incomes," *Econometrica*, Vol. 44, no. 51, September, pp. 963–970.

Stone, J. Richard. (1953). *The Measurement of Consumers' Expenditure and Behaviour in the United Kingdom, 1820–1938*, Vol. I. Cambridge: Cambridge University Press.

————.(1954). "Linear Expenditure Systems and Demand Analysis: An Application to the Pattern of British Demand," *Economic Journal*, Vol. 64, pp. 511–527.

Theil, Henri. (1971). *Principles of Econometrics*. New York: John Wiley & Sons, Inc.

Thurow, Lester. (1970). "Analyzing the American Income Distribution," *American Economic Review*, no. 60, pp. 261–270.

Tobin, James and Walter Dolde. (1971). "Wealth, Liquidity and Consumption" in *Consumer Spending and Monetary Policy: The Linkages, Proceedings of a Monetary Conference* held at Nantucket Island, Massachusetts, June. Boston: The Federal Reserve Bank of Boston.

Treyz, George, G. E. DuGuay, C. Lon Chen and Roy Williams. (1981). "A Family Distribution Model for Regional (Massachusetts) Policy Analysis," *Journal of Policy Modeling*, Vol. 3, pp. 77–92.

U.S. Bureau of the Census. (1960–1981). *Current Population Reports*, Series P-60, 1960–1981. Washington, D.C.: U.S. Government Printing Office.

U.S. Department of Labor, Bureau of Labor Statistics. (1978). *Consumer Expenditure Survey: Integrated Diary and Interview Survey Data, 1972–73*, Bulletin 1992. Washington, D.C.: U.S. Government Printing Office.

Varian, Hal R. (1978). *Microeconomic Analysis*. New York: W. W. Norton & Co.

Wharton Annual Model Alternative Scenarios. (1981). Philadelphia: Wharton Econometric Forecasting Associates.

Yaari, Menachem. (1976). "A Law of Large Numbers in the Theory of Consumer's Choice Under Uncertainty," *Journal of Economic Theory*, Vol. 12, April.

Index

Ability theory, 44
Ability-to-Pay principle, 1
Adjusted gross income, 85, 86
After-tax rate of return, 60, 62–63, 64, 132, 134, 138
Aggregation, 17–29, 32–33
Almon lag, 63

Bradley-Gephardt proposal, 3, 129, 135–39
Budget constraint, 9–10, 13, 60–61
Business fixed investment, 149, 154–55, 160

Capital stock, 148, 160
Civil War tax, 1
Coefficient of variation, 46
Colinearity, 34
Collector effect, 53
Consistent aggregation, 17–18, 35, 36
Consumer theory, 8–9, 40, 50
Consumer unit, 50
Consumption plan, 11
Cramer-Rao lower bound, 52
Cross section budget study, 33, 37, 43, 65, 71, 158

Demand analysis, 9, 15–16
Demand equation method, 34, 39–41, 58, 59, 66–71, 80, 86–87, 89, 106–7, 160
Demographics, 59, 100
Density functions, 45, 46
Disposable income, 59, 85, 86, 112, 114, 138, 141–43, 145

Economic Recovery Tax Act of 1981, 2, 157
Effective tax rates, 42, 54, 85, 109
Elementary good, 17, 18
Engel curves, 19, 20, 34, 40

Estimation bias, 66, 158
Estimation techniques, 20, 66
Euler's theorem, 52–53
Exact aggregation, 40
Existence, 27–28, 69
Expenditure ratio method, 34, 58, 59–61, 79–80, 88–89, 105–6, 160
Ex Ante tax rate, 145–50, 156
Ex Post tax rate, 150–55

Fisher two-period model, 9–12
Flat tax, 100, 129–56, 158, 159, 160

Gamma income distribution, 45, 46–47, 53, 107, 158
Generalized least squares, 67
Gini coefficient, 44, 45, 46, 47
Government deficit, 150, 155
Gross National Product (GNP), 145, 146, 152

Heteroscedastic errors, 66

Income distribution, 22, 32, 43–47, 49–53, 75–79, 87
Income elasticity, 41, 100, 102, 104, 105
Intertemporal allocation, 9

Joint simulation, 143–50

Kemp–Roth tax cuts, 113, 130
Keynesian multiplier, 103–4

Laffer curve, 130
Life cycle model, 22–24, 104
Lorenz curve, 44

Marginal propensity to consume, 61,
  100–101, 102, 105, 108, 123, 144
Marginal tax rates, 42, 157
Micro simulation, 27, 32–33, 38
Model simulation, 84
Money supply, 145, 148
Multi-period model, 12–15

Net foreign investment, 150

Ordinary least squares, 35, 67

Permanent income model, 22, 24–25, 37
Pooled data, 34
Population, 90
Preference ordering, 16
Price effects, 33, 58, 61

Reagan, Ronald, 129, 130
Representative consumer, 20, 33
Residential investment, 149, 154–55
Retained earnings, 150

Retirement, 13
Roy's Identity, 16

Savings, 11, 34, 66, 89, 114–15, 119, 134,
  143, 148–50, 157, 160
Sensitivity analysis, 39, 100, 117
Sixteenth Amendment, 1
Slutsky condition, 16
Social insurance, 112, 160
Stochastic theory of income distribution, 44
Structure of tax rates, 41–43, 136

Tax collections, 49–50, 54, 56–58, 85–86, 88
Tax deductions, 41–42, 132–33, 135
Time trend, 62, 63, 68
Trade balance, 148, 150
Transfer payments, 85–86

Utility maximization, 10, 36

Wharton Long-Term model, 131, 139, 145,
  148, 159, 160